CRAFT ACTIVISM

PEOPLE, IDEAS, AND PROJECTS
FROM THE NEW COMMUNITY OF HANDMADE
AND HOW YOU CAN JOIN IN

JOAN TAPPER   PHOTOGRAPHY BY GALE ZUCKER

FOREWORD BY FAYTHE LEVINE

POTTER
CRAFT

NEW YORK

CONTENTS

5 FOREWORD BY FAYTHE LEVINE

6 INTRODUCTION

PART I: CRAFTING A STATEMENT 8

KNIT BOMBING The JafaGirls 10
  13 **DIY**: Games of Tag
  14 **Makers Jam**
  15 **PROJECT**: Bench Warmer

QUILTS WITH A MESSAGE Carolyn Mazloomi 20
  23 **DIY**: Calculating the Value of Handmade
  24 **Makers Jam**
  25 **PROJECT**: Easy-Piecey Peace Quilt

**A KNITTED SPOTLIGHT
ON ENDANGERED SPECIES** Ruth Marshall 28
  31 **Makers Jam**
  32 **PROJECT**: Ocelot Scarf

ARTIST TRADING CARDS Bee Shay 36
  39 **DIY**: Hosting an ATC Meeting/Exchange
  40 **PROJECT**: Serendipity Artist Trading Card
  43 **DIY**: Become an Ambassador of Handmade

KNITTING IS POLITICAL Lisa Anne Auerbach 44
  47 **DIY**: Writing With Yarn
  48 **PROJECT**: Sharrow Cardi

PART II: RECRAFTING THE PAST 54

NOT YOUR GRANDMOTHER'S EMBROIDERY Jenny Hart 56
  59 **DIY**: It *Is* All About You
  60 **Makers Jam**
  61 **PROJECT**: Hot Stuff Stitching

A NEW TAKE ON OLD DOMESTIC ARTS
Catherine Clark and Katie Metzger 64
  67 **DIY**: Share Your Passion by Teaching
  68 **PROJECT**: Bella Brooklyn Housedress
  71 **DIY**: The Apron Revisited

RETURN OF THE GRANNY SQUARE Ellen Bloom 72
  75 **DIY**: How to Organize a Craft Night
  76 **Makers Jam**
  77 **PROJECT**: Granny GreenBag

PART III: CRAFTING FOR A CAUSE 80

KNITTERS UNITED The Red Scarf Project 82
  85 **DIY**: Think Local
  86 **Makers Jam**
  88 **PROJECT**: On the Quad Scarf
  90 **PROJECT**: Fussy Cuts Blanket
  98 **PROJECT**: Sleight of Hands Mittens

PART IV: CRAFTING TO RECYCLE, RENEW, AND REUSE 102

RECYCLED CHIC Crispina ffrench 104

107 **DIY**: Digging for Vintage Treasure

108 Makers Jam

109 **PROJECT**: Sun-Tea Dresses

ONE WORD: PLASTIC Virginia Fleck 112

114 **DIY**: Plabric Anyone?

115 Makers Jam

116 **PROJECT**: Tongue-in-Chic Skirt

TOYS OUT OF TRASH Loran Scruggs 120

122 **DIY**: Tin Envy

124 **PROJECT**: Fleur de Tin Can

PART V: CRAFTING A COMMUNITY 128

GET ORGANIZED The Ravelry Phenomenon 130

134 Makers Jam

136 **DIY**: How to Craft a Craft Fair

137 **PROJECT**: Craftitude Vest

142 **PROJECT**: Long Day to Starlit Night Wrap

147 **PROJECT**: Lounge Act Cardigan

HOW TO GET CRAFTING 152

153 KNITTING ABBREVIATIONS AND YARN WEIGHT CHART

154 SUGGESTED READING AND OTHER RESOURCES

157 ACKNOWLEDGMENTS

158 INDEX

FOREWORD BY Faythe Levine

DIRECTOR OF **HANDMADE NATION**

WHEN I AM ASKED TO DEFINE *CRAFT,* **I DON'T AND** I won't. I like to think of it as undefinable—with no rules—and that is why I was drawn to it in the first place. Craft is a way to connect with people, a way to create a community that you are inspired by. I have come to realize that once one's hands are in motion, "making" is difficult to stop. There may be long lapses, unfinished projects, even disasters, but the feeling inside you never leaves. Do you know the feeling I am talking about? The one that makes you relax, focus, and feel proud that you are making something? That is an example of the power of craft. Regardless of one's skill level, I truly believe that making things makes good.

While conducting interviews over the past few years, I must have asked hundreds of people the same question: "So, how long have you been making stuff?" Ask me, and my answer, like many of yours, is "I've always made things, ever since I was a little kid."

What I make now is films, and what I have made in the past runs the gamut of craft. My story would continue: "No, I didn't go to college. Yes, I make a 'living' as an independent artist. No, I'm not professionally trained. No, I don't currently have to support kids or pets. Yes, it's difficult to balance it all. Yes, I work *all* the time. And yes, I am very, very happy with my life."

Showing a flair for fashion, a model in the Tongue-in-Chic Skirt turns the head of ukulele busker Howlin' Hobbit on the streets of Seattle.

But that story is mine. The story of the girl next to me will be very different. So, too, the story of the guy next to her, and so on. That is what I love about this book: We get to see into the lives of others, to understand what motivates them. We all live very differently under the umbrella of craft, though we share a common bond of making and creating. It's who we are and will continue to be, as we grow old. Then another generation will come along and start it all over again. Or so we hope.

Living a DIY lifestyle is nothing new. Our generation's interest in the resurgence of craft started as a grassroots phenomenon, though now I think it's safe to say it's leaked into mainstream culture. We make to provide. We make to give. We make to share. We make because we love. Making is marketable, it's "green," it's local. And when the fad passes, we will still be making. Because making things by hand has never stopped, and it will never disappear.

When it comes to craft, I encourage you all to spend time observing and absorbing what's around you—in your personal lives and also what is available online. Be inspired by the amazing people and projects within this book. Make the ideas your own, use the resources as a springboard, and then share your story with others. Remember, the empowerment of craft is contagious.

INTRODUCTION

IN 2008, I HAPPENED TO VISIT LA CONNOR, Washington, a small, artsy community with several museums, a smattering of galleries, and a healthy program of outdoor sculpture. The latter included a statue of a gone-but-not-forgotten town canine known as Dirty Biter, whose sleek bronze body was wrapped in a handcrafted sweater. The garment was the work of a "drive-by knitter," I heard, who had also placed boalike scarves around the neck of *Silent Words*, another sculpted figure across the street. No, no one knew who the nameless needleworker was, the woman in the local yarn store told me, which may or may not have been true. But that was my first experience with knit bombing—tagging trees, poles, and other public spots with knit or crocheted swatches.

Boy, was I ever intrigued. Among the questions that fascinated me (along with the obvious, "Didn't anyone see the person do it?") were: Why would someone do such a thing? And how? Overall, though, my reaction was: This is a great idea . . . and a very funny one. As I began to read about knit bombing (also known as yarn bombing), I realized that it was a worldwide movement with warm and cozy, if sometimes gargantuan, results. Knit bombers have covered a bridge in Ontario, an artist named Magda Sayeg

had tagged the Great Wall of China, and statues have been seen wearing scarves from Europe to Australia, prompting me to wonder, how is it that knitting has emerged from one's sitting room onto a broader stage?

Later I came to realize that all kinds of crafts have moved from personal passion to public statement. Think of the impact the AIDS quilt has made over the last twenty-five years. More recently, makers have come up with all kinds of clever ideas to be eco-friendly, including reusable bags—made of fabric, recycled plastic, and yarn, to name just a few—as part of an energetic campaign to do away with the ubiquitous plastic grocery bag.

As photographer Gale Zucker and I met and talked to crafters, many of whom are featured in this book, we were stunned to realize how far-reaching this new blend of craft and activism— what writer Betsy Greer has called "craftivism"— really is. It affects what people make, why they make it, what they make it out of, and whom they tell about it. It's part of the DIY movement, which promotes handmade objects (and a lifestyle that goes with them) over mass-produced articles. And the work as been enriched by formally trained artists who are embracing age-old crafts. The irony, of course, is that the new directions, popularity, and even profitability of the work of one's own hands and heart have been expanded by the most up-to-date technology, in particular, by the Internet.

By connecting makers with those who share their enthusiasms, the Web has altered the crafting landscape, allowing the viral spread of ideas and techniques, creating a far-reaching community, mobilizing like-minded people in support of causes, and opening global doors to those whose work might once have been noticed only in their hometown.

All that begins, though, with the magic of an individual's vision and skill. Why focus on the particular makers in this book? Because they excited us, and we believed the story behind them and their creations would excite and inspire you, too. Carolyn Mazloomi's quilts, for example, are stunning graphic art, but how much more powerful to know she taught herself to quilt and then set out to tell what she felt were important stories with her craft. And what about the granny squares that Ellen Bloom has taught scores of Los Angeles crafters to make? After seeing her personal granny square suite, I'm sure neither Gale nor I will ever think of crochet in quite the same way again. And remember those plastic bags? We were amazed by the way Virginia Fleck has turned advertising messages into her jaw-dropping designs.

The artists and crafters we've chosen use many kinds of media and have a variety of goals in mind, but similar themes surface again and again: Crafting a Statement (Part I) focuses on political comments, broadly defined as statements that may highlight political opinions, social issues, endangered animals, or the use of art for art's sake. Recrafting the Past (Part II) points out the way traditional pursuits like embroidery, sewing, and crochet have returned with a new, spirited point of view and touches on the changing definition of feminism. Crafting for a Cause (Part III) examines that widespread, and time-honored, practice of creating to help others; while Crafting to Recycle, Renew, and Reuse (Part IV) covers crafters who've gone green. Finally, Crafting a Community (Part V) explores how we forge bonds with other like-minded makers nearby or around the globe.

Along with the profiles are projects from or inspired by the makers, as well as tips, hints, ideas, and resources to move you to action. There's also a list of Web links to connect you even farther. The lives and work of the people in this book make a statement about the power of craft. You can, too.

—Joan Tapper

PART I

CRAFTING A

A sweater with a slogan. A quilt that's a call to action. A publicly displayed swatch of knitting that unites a community with its spirit of pure fun. What's going on?

Something new has entered the world of craft. The age-old question used to be: Is it utilitarian or is it art? Well, we can still cherish our handmade sweaters, mittens, or quilts as winter wear and warm coverings for a bed. And we can marvel at an exquisite woven rug hanging in a gallery as a piece of purely decorative art. But now these handmade objects may be something more—not only the outpouring of an artist's personal vision but also a point of view that's designed to persuade us.

Now we can go to quilt exhibits that bring issues to our attention with artistry that often has tangible fund-raising results. We can find comments on politics woven into gorgeous garments or incorporated into environmental installations that are meant to provoke a dialogue. An exhibit of crafts that use animal skin patterns can startle those of us who may never have thought about endangered species into taking action to save

STATEMENT

the world's big cats. Even the act of exchanging a tiny handcrafted collage or placing a knitted tag in a tree may help us forge bonds, with individuals or groups, where none existed before.

The goal is to make us all start talking—and keep talking—about art, about politics, about one's place in a community.

KNIT BOMBING

THE JAFAGIRLS

SPRING FLOWERS WERE BLOOMING IN YELLOW Springs, Ohio, which was hardly a surprise until you consider that the flowers were made of felt with buttons, beads, and lace, and they were bursting forth not in gardens but on telephone poles, benches, trees, and banisters. This was a display of "Flower Power," an outpouring of community textile graffiti, led by "knit bombers" Corrine Bayraktaroglu and Nancy Mellon, otherwise known as the JafaGirls.

The two women have been installing their creations on the streets of their town since 2007, when they organized a street-art-themed event for the Yellow Springs Arts Council. Researching the topic, Corrine came across pictures of knit tags by Magda Sayeg, a noted knit bomber based in Austin. Suddenly a bare tree outside their venue looked full of possibilities. "Nancy said, 'I think *it* should have some knitting,'" Corrine remembers. So they joined the burgeoning knit bombing movement by attaching a couple of knit swatches to the trunk.

"The public response was phenomenal," she says. They dubbed their creation the Knit Knot Tree, and it stayed up for months, embellished

from time to time with additions by the JafaGirls and anonymous contributions.

Corrine, who was born in the northeast of England, came to Yellow Springs as a newlywed with her husband in 1978 and, after years of moving around, returned to Ohio in 2002. She says her grandmothers and mother taught her to knit, crochet, and embroider, but when her son was born twenty-seven years ago, followed by a daughter two years later, she had little time for crafts. About fifteen years ago she turned to fine art, which she uses "to explore questions and issues that concern me, confound me, please me, and interest me."

Suddenly a bare tree outside their venue looked full of possibilities.

And the name *JafaGirls*? That was the result of an ill-attended opening of one of her exhibits in an off-the-beaten-track gallery. Her husband observed, "Maybe they think you're just a bunch of Jafas," as in "Just Another F*#&@*%g Artist." "Yes, we're Jafas," Corrine responded, "and I'm not going to follow the rules anymore."

In Nancy Mellon she found a kindred spirit. Nancy grew up in Park Ridge, Illinois, and remembers visiting her grandmother in

CLOCKWISE FROM TOP LEFT: Corrine Bayraktaroglu in her studio; Corrine, Nancy Mellon, and their bench; a flower power welcome to Yellow Springs; the JafaGirls with Mr. Plato; the Knit Knot tree.

Knit bombers in downtown Yellow Springs give peace a chance by covering a telephone pole with symbols and swatches. The JafaGirls and other crafty citizens also brought Flower Power to public spaces.

Pennsylvania, whose huge cabinets were filled with stuffed animals and crazy quilts. She learned to embroider (but hated following patterns), met her husband in Chicago, tried "the acting thing in New York," and lived for a time in California. Eventually, they wanted to go back to the Midwest. With their two teenage sons, the couple sought out attractive art towns; Yellow Springs was a "wonderful" choice.

The JafaGirls now meet every Tuesday to dream up projects and put them together, sometimes over the course of months. Among their creations is "Mr. Plato," a felt-covered, life-size resuscitation doll destined for a spot on a public bench. ("In Yellow Springs there are lots of philosophers who sit on benches," Nancy explains.) There has been a considerable amount of yarn bombing, too: a "Nosy Tree" decorated with plaster casts of locals' shnozzes; an all-red "Queen of Hearts Tree"; a "Bumble Bee Pole," featuring felt bumble bees; and mixed-media adornments for "Elaine's Bench," which memorialized a cherished member of the Yellow Springs community.

The two are part of a global network of knit bombers, many of whom tag surreptitiously, in the dark of night. "We stay in touch with Grrl+Dog in Australia, Knit the City in London, and Yarn Bombing in Canada," says Corrine. But they've given up trying to "do things sneakily. In a village of 3,500, it's hard to be anonymous."

Besides, they relish the reactions of their fellow citizens. "That's our favorite part," says Nancy. "When we are out working, people stop and talk and give us a thumbs-up." Even the local police have been known to pitch in, by helping to put a knit covering in a hard-to-reach spot.

A stitch in time attaches the Bench Warmer in place.

D.I.Y. *Games of Tag*

If you think your local trees, telephone poles, and street signs look as though they need a little something, you (and perhaps a few fiber-oriented friends) might consider yarn bombing. Here are tips from the JafaGirls.

KNOW YOUR AREA and be prepared for a wide range of reactions. In usually liberal Berkeley, California, a cozy on a public sculpture brought a demand that the defacing object be removed, while in Britain, Knit the City yarn bombers covering a phone booth near Parliament were spotted by a bobby, who noted that since his wife was a knitter, he wouldn't arrest them. If the object to be tagged is on private property, you may want to ask permission.

TAKE A QUICK MEASUREMENT of the object to be covered.

TREAT KNIT OR CROCHETED TAGS IN ADVANCE with a waterproofing/UV-protecting product (Granger's Soft Shell UV Proof, for example). This will help keep the work from fading or deteriorating too fast. Felt tags should be treated with a UV-resistant fabric spray.

BRING SELF-ADHESIVE VELCRO and a small pair of scissors.

KEEP THE TAG SEVERAL FEET (1m or so) off the ground. Dogs like to leave their marks.

IF THE ART IS MEANT TO HIGHLIGHT AN ISSUE, leave a tag with a link to a URL where someone could find out more. If you don't care about remaining anonymous, sign your name.

GIVE CREDIT to people who add things to the street art. That contributes to a sense of community.

FINALLY, ALWAYS CARRY A CAMERA to document the event!

For "Flower Power," they counted on the contributions of many other crafters. "I wanted to cover a telephone pole with flowers," Corrine remembers, "but Nancy said, 'I don't see how we can do it.'" Eventually, about fifteen people—men, women, and children—met once a week at a coffee shop, and the project evolved into using the flowers—four hundred in all—in various spots around town.

"I love treating the outside as our gallery," Corrine says. "I love to see the public laughing and touching things. And I like it when you can incorporate something into the piece that someone else has made."

"Visual art is lonely," Nancy adds. "You work by yourself. This has given us a wonderful playful relationship with the community."

Makers Jam

A number of serious fiber artists have moved on from telephone poles and trees to a few bigger things—like gas stations, water towers, and woodland paths.

ROBYN LOVE'S *The Knitted Mile*, a strip of yellow knitting produced by ninety craftspeople from all over North America, unrolled down a mile (1.6km) of highway in Dallas, Texas. With a half-dozen master crocheters, Robyn, a resident of Newfoundland, Canada, also turned a water tower atop a sixteen-story building in New York's SoHo into a yarn-sheathed "pencil"—in honor of a pencil-shaped art-and-design award.

CAROL HUMMEL'S crocheted installations often rest on strong philosophical bases. Her *Aspen Invasion—Steamboat Springs* showed off dozens of purple, orange, and yellow "stepping-stones" that meandered through the Colorado woods from hot tub to hot tub. Why? By commenting on "the abundance of condominiums that are proliferating on the aspen-covered mountains," she writes, the "piece highlights the challenges of population growth, consumerism, and environmental protection."

Artist **JENNIFER MARSH** founded the International Fiber Collaborative in 2007 to promote art and education. In 2008, she got students, individuals, and groups from fifteen countries and twenty-eight states to crochet, knit, stitch, patch, or collage 3-foot (.28m²) squares that she used to cover an abandoned gas station in New York State. She's really taking off with her next endeavor. For the *Dream Rocket*, in 2011, she'll wrap a replica of a *Saturn V* rocket in Huntsville, Alabama.

BENCH WARMER

DESIGNED BY Corrine Bayraktaroglu and Nancy Mellon   **SKILL LEVEL** Easy

The JafaGirls designed this project for a bench that bears a memorial plaque for a warmly remembered local citizen, but you can add it straight across the top slat of any bench that you feel needs some character. The designers couple their signature felt appliqué with knit and crocheted segments and sew in beads, buttons, and other small meaningful tokens.

FINISHED MEASUREMENTS

To fit top bar of bench: 95" x 11"
(241.5cm x 28cm),
or to your measurements

MATERIALS

1 yd (91cm) black felt

7–8 felt pieces in assorted colors
(the JafaGirls used 9" x 12" [23cm
x 30.5cm] pieces by Eco-fi, made
from recycled postconsumer plastic
bottles)

Embroidery floss in assorted colors

3 small buttons, assorted

Scrap yarn in assorted types and colors

UV Fabric Spray

TOOLS

Tracing paper

Pinking shears

Scissors

Sewing supplies: needle, heavy-duty
thread, sewing pins

Size U.S. 10 (6mm) straight knitting
needles

Size U.S. I-9 (5.5mm) crochet hook

Tapestry needle

Flat, stiff board to push the felt between
the slats

THE BENCH

Felt 7 ½" (19cm) wide	Knit & Crochet 21" (53.5cm) wide	Felt 39" (99cm) wide	Knit & Crochet 21" (53.5cm) wide	Felt 7 ½" (19cm) wide

1. Pick out your bench and measure it. Your felt panels should be made 1½" (3.8cm) larger in circumference than the bench slat. Knit panels should be made ½–1" (13mm–2.5cm) larger in circumference than the bench slat. In length, plan out the size of your sections so that the total length is about 1" (2.5cm) longer than your slat. This will allow for a ½" (13mm) turn under on the far ends of the left and right felt sections.

2. At home, cut out one pair of Felt End Panel pieces and the Felt Center Panel piece out of the felt yardage. Turn under ½" (13mm) along the opposite long edges of the End Panels and stitch with floss. This creates a nice finish on the outside ends of the piece.

3. Create felt panel appliqués.

NOTE: The leaves and flowers are made of multiple layers of felt. Study each pattern to determine the various layers, and then trace each

layer separately. Trace and then cut out each layer in the desired color of felt.

LARGE ROUND 3-LAYER FLOWER (MAKE 1)

Trace or copy the Large 3-Layer Flower template.

Pick out a different color of felt for each layer. Using the template, cut out the 3 layers in felt. Cut out the middle circle with pinking shears.

Layer, starting with the flower piece on the bottom, followed by the large circle, and top with the small circle.

Anchor all 3 layers with 6 French knots sewn through the center of the top circle. Stitch around the top circle, using long stitches radiating from the outer edge of the top circle to the outer edge of the middle circle.

SMALL SQUARE 4-LAYER FLOWER (MAKE 5)

Trace or copy the 4-Layer Flower template. Pick out a different color of felt for each layer. Using the template, cut out the 4 layers in felt. Cut out the 2nd layer square with pinking shears.

Layer, starting with the large square, then the smaller square, followed by the flower, and topped with the circle.

Anchor all 4 layers by stitching around the circle, through all layers. Radiate 3 stitches—short, long, short—on each petal.

SMALL ROUND 6-LAYER FLOWER (MAKE 3)

Trace or copy the 6-Layer Flower template.

Pick out 4 different colors of felt, 3 different colors of floss, and a small button.

Using the template, cut out the 6 layers in felt. Cut the 2nd and 4th layer circles with pinking shears. Layer, as shown in drawing, topping with a button. Stitch the button through all layers to anchor the flower together. Stitch around top circle. Stitch around petals using a running stitch.

SMALL 3-LAYER LEAF
AND LARGE 3-LAYER LEAF
(MAKE 5 SMALL AND 6 LARGE LEAVES)

Trace or copy the 3-Layer Leaf and the Large 3-Layer Leaf template.

Pick out different colors of felt for each layer.

Cut 5 (for small leaf) of each layer using pinking shears.

Cut 6 (for large leaf) of each layer using pinking shears.

Layer leaves with a bottom leaf, a middle leaf, and a top leaf.

Using assorted colors of floss, stitch through all 3 layers to make the top stem design on the top leaf and to anchor the leaf together.

Stitch around the middle layer to the bottom layer. (It's fun to use different-colored floss for each layer.)

4. Pin each of the finished flowers to the Center, Left, and Right Felt Panels, following the diagram for placement.

NOTES: For the 3-Layer Flower, stitch the base flower to the background felt using a running stitch around each petal.

For the 4-Layer Flower, stitch around the bottom square to anchor it to the felt background.

For the 6-Layer Flower, stitch around the bottom circle to anchor it to the felt background.

For the leaves, stitch around the bottom to anchor them to the felt background.

5. Spray the completed felt panels with UV spray.

6. Make the knit and crocheted panels.

Knit panels using either garter or stockinette stitch, or crochet granny squares in various widths and join together, to create 2 panels that measure 21" x 12" (53.5cm x 30.5cm) each. Use various types and colors of yarn.

TIP: If the yarn stretches too much, you can always unstitch a piece to shorten the length. If the yarn section is too short, bring along extra pieces of knitting/crochet to add.

7. Assemble the piece on the bench.

Start by attaching the Center Panel. Push the bottom edge of the panel under the top slat, using a piece of thin board. Stand behind the bench to sew it on using heavy-duty thread. Turn the top edge of your felt under and sew it over the bottom edge. Pull the 2 ends snug against the slat, so it won't revolve.

8. Position the knit and crocheted panels on either end of Center Panel. Using a whipstitch, sew onto the slat, then sew to the Center Panel.

TIP: Use a tapestry needle and yarn or strong thread; embroidery floss or regular thread won't hold up.

same way you did the Center Panel. Then stitch them to the end of the knitted pieces.

10. Take plenty of time to enjoy the process and to make friends.

If this isn't an anonymous piece, add a small name tag to your work. Corrine usually cuts a felt rectangle with pinking shears, and embroiders *JafaGirls* on it.

NOTES: You can choose whether to preattach the flowers and leaves, as we've described, or you can do this on site. If you wait to attach the flowers until you are on site and have stitched on the background felt, you will have more control in the placement of the flowers. Bring a kit with yarn and large tapestry needles, black yarn/heavy-duty thread, scissors, and UV fabric spray for felt. Depending on how much sun it gets, your piece will last 3 months to a year.

LARGE 3-LAYER FLOWER

5"

ENLARGE ALL
TEMPLATES
135%

LARGE 3-LAYER LEAF

3½"

SMALL 3-LAYER LEAF

2 ¾"

FELT END PANEL
Cut 1 face-up for Right End
Cut 1 face-down for Left End

7 ½"

12 ½"

*Square flower
placement*

Fold line for turn-under

SMALL SQUARE 4-LAYER FLOWER

2 ½"

2 ½"

SMALL 6-LAYER FLOWER

2 ¾"

CENTER FELT PANEL,
showing flower and leaf placement, cut 1

39"

12 ½"

QUILTS WITH A MESSAGE

CAROLYN MAZLOOMI

WHEN CAROLYN MAZLOOMI WAS ASKED TO co-curate a quilt exhibit to honor President Barack Obama's inauguration, she knew she wanted something more than a conventional series of textile portraits. And she knew just how to get it. She invited forty-four members of the Women of Color Quilters' Network—Obama being the forty-fourth president—to contribute a work. She specifically asked for quilts that reflected how Obama became president. "We've walked the journey through racism," Carolyn says. "I wanted the artists to go deep and talk about that journey."

Her own quilt for the exhibit, which is documented in her book *Journey of Hope*, is a graphically bold depiction of protest marchers set against a map of Selma to Montgomery, Alabama. It not only highlights a landmark of the civil rights movement but also underscores the importance of narrative quilts in the African American tradition.

In fact, the first quilts Carolyn made, in the early 1980s, were black-and-white narrative quilts that looked a lot like linocuts. "They were stark," she remembers, "with no color to get in the way."

It was a departure that she began quilting

CLOCKWISE FROM TOP LEFT: Carolyn Mazloomi quilting; a detail of a quilt in her collection; trimming threads; two examples of her artistry—*Second Time Around* and *Ain't Gonna Let Nobody Turn Me Around*.

at all. Born in Louisiana, Carolyn was an aeronautical engineer, married to another aeronautical engineer whom she met in college. No one in her family sewed or fostered any kind of artistic talent. "They were just trying to survive," she adds.

But in the 1970s she came across traditional patchwork quilts from Appalachia, which were beginning to be marketed. "There was something mesmerizing about the quilts," she says. "And I vowed to teach myself to sew. It became an all-consuming passion."

> *"Quilting has been a way for women to discuss events and commune with each other."*

Carolyn taught herself the craft from a book, first quilting by hand and later using a sewing machine. From the beginning, she loved the feel of the fabric: "It's very satisfying to work with the cloth—which surrounds us when we're born and when we die." It's "a spiritual relationship," she adds. "When we create something, it's spirit-guided. It comes anointed."

At that time she was traveling for her job, and as her interest in the craft grew, she visited quilt shops wherever she went. "I never saw black quilters, though," she remembers. "Where

Amid an exhibit of their own Obama-themed art, Carolyn poses with fellow quilters at the National Afro-American Museum and Cultural Center in Wilberforce, Ohio.

were they? I put an ad in the *Quilters Newsletter* magazine and asked any African American quilters to call or write me. I got nine responses. We all were quilting in isolation, thinking we were the last of a dying breed."

By the mid-1980s the connection with those nine women had turned into the Women of Color Quilters' Network (WCQN). "It started as an educational network," she says. Though improvised quilts—colorful, often geometric, designs done without a pattern—were becoming collectible and shown in galleries, the women who made them often didn't receive fair compensation. "We needed to educate quilters about the monetary value and also the cultural significance." For WCQN, which eventually grew to about eighteen hundred members, she documented works, took photos, and even helped quilters sell their work.

Meanwhile, she felt improvised quilts "didn't define the breadth and depth of African American quilts, which, in reality, are just as varied as the community itself." So Carolyn took on the challenge of demonstrating other aspects of African American quilting, particularly its contemporary designs: "My charge is noting its place in American history."

As part of that mission, she frequently curates exhibits, like the Obama show, often around a theme such as African American women's history; spirituality, which underlined *Threads of Faith*; or jazz, which was the basis of *Textural Rhythms*. One outcome of the *Textural Rhythms* exhibit was that the minister of culture of Costa Rica heard about the exhibit, was "blown away by the quilts," and asked Carolyn to curate a show of African American quilters in his Central American country. That, in turn, led to an educational outreach program for women in Limon, Costa Rica, something the WCQN has done in other places as well.

For the past two decades, Carolyn and her husband have lived in Ohio, where they raised three sons. She's turned the basement of her home into a studio with ample space for her quilts, shelves of rare, antique fabric, and beadwork collections.

For her own creations, which sell in the five figures, there's a waiting list of collectors, but she also owns about seven hundred quilts by others—"narrative to abstract, improvised and art quilts. It's a big responsibility because they have to be safeguarded for the next generation."

"Craft is a social form," she says, and "quilting has been a way for women to get together to discuss events, disseminate information, and commune with each other. When you get a gathering of women, it's like a homecoming, a reunion. It's powerful."

Paintings about jazz liven the walls of Carolyn's studio. where she also displays symbolic beadwork headdresses from the Yoruba tribe in Africa.

Makers Jam

Award-winning photojournalist **ROLAND FREEMAN**, co-curator of the Obama quilt exhibits and founder/president of the Group for Cultural Documentation, has highlighted African American quilters in his book *Something to Keep You Warm: The Roland Freeman Collection of Black American Quilts from the Mississippi Heartland*, which accompanied a Smithsonian exhibition in 1979. He returned to that dimension of African American culture in 1996 with *A Communion of the Spirits: African-American Quilters, Preservers, and Their Stories*.

Among the quilters Roland has photographed is **GWENDOLYN MAGEE**, whose work explores the experiences of African Americans, from the degradation, violence, and despair of slavery to hopes for the future.

Filmmaker **LAUREN CROSS** contributes to the dialogue with her documentary, *The Skin Quilt Project*, which uses interviews with and stories of African American quilters to grapple with the issue of skin color politics and the way quilting empowers self-confidence within the community.

EASY-PIECEY PEACE QUILT

DESIGNED BY Carolyn Mazloomi   **SKILL LEVEL** Easy

Carolyn came up with a simple quilted project that even a beginner can make with ease. Stitch this statement with minimal piecing, and easily transferable images and words, to create a small wall hanging with a message.

FINISHED MEASUREMENTS

30 ½" x 30 ½" (77.5 x 77.5cm)

MATERIALS

Peace design template

1 piece 24 ½" x 24 ½" (62cm x 62cm) cotton fabric for front

1 yd (91cm) cotton fabric for border, cut into 2 strips 3 ½" x 24½" (9cm x 62.5cm) and 2 strips 3 ½" x 30½" (9cm x 78cm)

Textile paints (available in craft stores)

32½" x 32½" (82.5cm x 82.5cm) cotton batting

1 piece 32½" x 32 ½" (82.5cm x 82.5cm) cotton fabric for backing

1 piece 2" x 30" (5cm x 76cm) cotton fabric for a hanging sleeve (optional)

Fabric piece for binding, approximately 1½" (3.8cm) wide and at least 126" (3.2m) long (It can match the front or be a contrasting color.)

Thread in a color that matches the front

TOOLS

Fabric marker

Sewing machine

Small safety pins

Sewing needle

SEAM ALLOWANCE

¼" (6mm)

1. Bring the Peace Design template to a copy shop and have it enlarged to fit a 24" x 24" (61cm x 61cm) piece of paper.

2. Choose a fabric for the front of the quilt. The quilt shown has cotton fabric hand-dyed a sky blue.

3. Place the template under the fabric on a light table and trace the design onto the fabric using a fabric marker. If you do not have a light table, tape the design to a sunny window, then tape the fabric over it and trace.

4. Using textile paints, color in the birds, the peace sign, the olive branches, and the lettering. Heat-set the paint by ironing the fabric on the wrong side, following directions on the package.

5. Take the 3½" x 24½" (9cm x 62cm) fabric pieces and sew them to the top and bottom of the front of the quilt, right sides together. Sew the 3½" x 30½" (9cm x 77.5cm) pieces of fabric to either side of the fabric square, right sides together.

6. Assemble the quilt. Place the fabric backing piece right side down, and lay the cotton batting over it. On top, center the front of the quilt, right side up. The back and batting should be about 2" (5cm) larger than the top, since the quilting may stretch the top somewhat.

Pin the 3 layers together with small safety pins to stabilize them.

7. Using a thread that matches the quilt top, outline the peace symbol and the doves with machine stitching. If you wish, you may also outline the leaves. Then stipple the entire quilt top—that is, use meandering stitching. As you quilt, the top may stretch slightly. Trim the excess batting and backing so that all 3 pieces line up along the edges and are squared up.

8. Use the border strips to bind the piece on all 4 sides: Sew 1 edge of the binding to the quilt front, right sides together with a ¼" (6mm) seam allowance, mitering at the corners. Wrap the binding around the raw edge of the quilt. Turn under ¼" (6mm) on the opposite edge of the binding. Adjust so the turned-under edge just covers previous stitching. Pin in place and stitch from the right side, being careful to sew through the lower edge of the binding on the back.

9. Make the quilt sleeve (optional). If you wish to hang the quilt, use the 2" x 30" (5cm x 76cm) fabric strip to create a sleeve on the back. Turn under ½" (13mm) on all sides of the strip and press. Center the strip just below the top edge on the back. Hand-stitch the long ends to the backside of the quilt.

why not give peace a chance? why not give peace a chance? why not give peace a chance? why not give peace a chance?

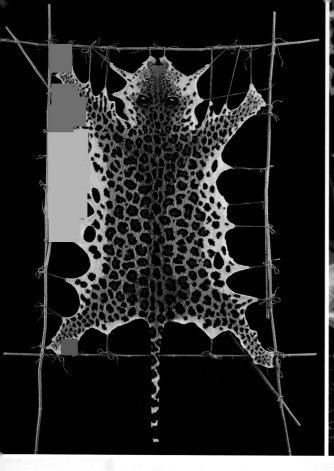

A KNITTED SPOTLIGHT ON ENDANGERED SPECIES

RUTH MARSHALL

IN A GALLERY, RUTH MARSHALL'S KNITTED sculptures of ocelots and jaguars stand out as framed, lit, provocative statements about animal conservation, meant to galvanize concern for the future of these beautiful endangered cats. She portrays reptiles, too. At her Bronx, New York, apartment-cum-workspace, she'll open a metal suitcase to reveal her suite of sixty-eight kinds of coral snakes, which looks like a display of men's neckwear, she jokes. In reality, it's an artistic interpretation of a collection of exotic specimens.

Ruth knit the snakes in 2006, working her way alphabetically through the species, which have an exquisite range of sizes and patterned bands of red, white, yellow, and black. "The serpents are mostly New World snakes—all venomous," she says, "and they live in forests and dense swamps." Her representations, based on meticulously gathered scientific information, are both gorgeous and accurate down to the embroidered brown dots on her favorite *Micrurus langsdorffi*.

There are no coral snakes in Australia, where Ruth was born and where she went to art

school. When she won a scholarship to continue her studies overseas, she chose Pratt Institute in New York, earned an MFA, and saw a posting for a job at the Bronx Zoo for an exhibit sculptor to work on the Congo Gorilla Forest, which re-created the environment in which the apes lived. The work only heightened her interest in wildlife conservation.

"The art was a dream come true," she remembers. "The animals were a bonus." Ruth spent the next fourteen years at the zoo, working on Tiger Mountain, refurbishing the World

Each tiger piece represents an animal that is alive and in the wild.

of Birds, and lending a hand in creating and maintaining the new Madagascar exhibit.

So how did she get from sculpting rain forest environments to knitting snakes and endangered large cats? "I was taught by my mother and aunt," she says, "and I knitted clothes for my dolls and finished sweaters for my brothers."

Though there were years when she had no time for the craft, she picked it up again in the early 2000s, on a trip back to Australia. "I started

CLOCKWISE FROM TOP LEFT: Ruth Marshall's knitted, framed *Amur Leopard*; Ruth working on a chart with feline inspiration; a sketchbook page; ocelot-patterned stitches; examining a pelt.

Art meets science as Ruth works in the archives of the Yale Peabody Museum of Natural History.

socks," she says, which were small and very sculptural. "I knitted socks for the whole family."

When she returned to New York, Ruth kept on knitting, occasionally taking her projects to the zoo. When she "was given an assignment to fabricate a Gaboon viper in urethane, embedded in concrete, and painted to look real, my boss joked, 'OK, you should knit that.' It was a lightbulb moment."

By 2002, she had embraced the challenge. "The Gaboon viper, one of the most venomous snakes in the world, is five to six feet [1.5–1.8m] long, gray and buff, with pinks and yellow. I made a chart and then knitted it flat."

Emboldened, Ruth wanted to tackle big cats, like the snow leopard, whose living area backed up

to her workspace. But the next animal she actually committed to wool was smaller and friendlier—her pet cat, Rocky. After that, Ruth went on to the snow leopard, the coral snakes, and other large cats, like jaguars, leopards, ocelots, and now tigers.

Having learned over the years that every animal is an individual, Ruth often begins by studying a specific pelt. She'll trace the skin, bring in yarn samples, take photos, and make sketches. Then she draws a chart to scale on graph paper. Sitting in a comfortable armchair and using a standing magnifying glass to follow the intricate pattern, she'll begin at the tail and use circular needles to produce the stunning stranded colorwork.

The finished work is often exhibited lashed onto a frame fashioned of sticks, which makes a statement about the poaching that makes these animals increasingly rare. Gallery-goers are frequently surprised. "They don't realize the animal was this big, or how complicated their patterns are," Ruth says. Or that the cats may be threatened.

She's currently finishing a series of six ocelots, and exhibits are scheduled for the future. But Ruth has something even more ambitious in mind—a Tiger Pelt Project, in which each new piece represents an animal that is alive and living in the wild. "There are only 3,500 wild tigers left," she says. "I'll make a work of art based on a scientist's pictures and measurements. Only when scientists can study multiple individual tigers can they gather enough data to understand the species and come up with conservation strategies." Her knitted tigers are a way for her to dramatize the big cats' plight to other crafters.

In the meantime, though, Marshall marvels when she considers the knitted animals she's produced. "I never thought I'd live in New York or work at a zoo," she says. "You start going on a certain journey in life, and you never know where it will take you."

Makers Jam

Spurred by the effects of global warming on ocean temperatures and the health of coral reefs, in 2005 **CHRISTINE AND MARGARET WERTHEIM** founded the Hyperbolic Crochet Coral Reef Project, an innovative—and visually spectacular—combination of community art with science.

Using the art of crochet, and under the auspices of their Institute for Figuring in Los Angeles, the Australian-born twin sisters are modeling forms of hyperbolic geometry through the craft, which happens to be the only way to demonstrate those mathematical principles, and at the same time demonstrating the power of feminine handicrafts.

Over the last five years, Christine and Margaret, with the help of some 2,500 contributors around the world, have replicated corals, kelps, sea slugs, sponges, and other marine creatures in startlingly lifelike and ever-growing reefs that fill entire galleries and display spaces in New York, Chicago, London, Los Angeles, Scottsdale, Dublin, and, most recently, the Smithsonian's Natural History Museum in Washington, D.C. In conjunction with their exhibits, which have drawn crowds of thirty thousand in places, they have helped create workshops that teach the art of hyperbolic crochet and have given rise to community-based crocheted coral reefs.

A former park ranger, San Francisco artist **LAUREL ROTH** says she uses "art as a medium to examine the biological ramifications of human behavior." One recent series of works, she notes, has as its springboard women's traditional fiber crafts. In this case, Laurel has knitted and crocheted urban pigeons that give them new identities as extinct birds. Both whimsical and artistic, her fiber craft sculpture reminds us that the Carolina parakeet, the dodo, the passenger pigeon, and perhaps the ivory-billed woodpecker are no longer on Earth.

OCELOT SCARF

DESIGNED BY Ruth Marshall and Dorothy Orzel   **SKILL LEVEL** Experienced

Ruth Marshall's knitted reproductions of animal skins have been exhibited as fine art, but she worked with Dorothy Orzel to transform her chart of an ocelot's coat into this gorgeous scarf. The scarf is knit in stockinette stitch except for a small (3-stitch) seed stitch border all around. The pattern is worked using the stranded colorwork method of carrying yarns across the back. The silk lining covers the floats in back, producing a polished and elegant wearable piece.

FINISHED MEASUREMENTS

6" x 72" (15cm x 183cm)

MATERIALS

2 skeins Berroco Ultra Alpaca Light, 50% Super Fine Alpaca, 50% Peruvian Wool, 1¾ oz (50g), 144 yd (133m), in Winter White (A)

2 skeins Berroco Ultra Alpaca Light, 50% Super Fine Alpaca 50% Peruvian Wool, 1¾ oz (50g), 144 yd (133m), in Tupelo (B)

1 skein Berroco Ultra Alpaca Light, 50% Super Fine Alpaca, 50% Peruvian Wool, 1¾ oz (50g), 144 yd (133m) in Pitch Black (C)

1 skein Berroco Ultra Alpaca Light, 50% Super Fine Alpaca, 50% Peruvian Wool, 1¾ oz (50g), 144 yd (133m) in Mahogany Mix (D)

2 FINE

½ yd (45.5cm) crepe de chine fabric, 100% silk, 45" (114cm) width

TOOLS

Size U.S. 5 (3.75mm) needles, or size to obtain gauge
Scissors
Sewing machine or needle and thread
Fabric marker or tailor's chalk
Iron
Sewing pins
Sewing needle
Thread to match fabric

GAUGE

23 stitches and 32 rows = 4" (10 cm) in multicolored pattern

SEED STITCH: A pattern of alternating knit and purl stitches. When the stitch you are working into presents as a knit stitch, you purl into it. When it presents as a purl, you knit into it.

STRANDED COLORWORK: Knitting using two or more colors to create a pattern. One color is used to form the stitch while the other colors are carried behind on the wrong side of the work as "floats." It's important to keep the tension loose on the floats to prevent pulling. Check online resources for other tips when using this method.

BACKWARD LOOP INCREASE: A method of adding a stitch. Wind the yarn from back to front over your left index finger. Insert the right needle from right to left into the front of the loop, transferring the stitch to the right needle. Pull loop snug.

SCARF

Cast on 7 stitches with A.

OCELOT CHART

Starting with Row 1, work the ocelot chart in as indicated. The backward loop method of increasing works well for this project.

FINISHING

Bind off all stitches and weave in ends. Gently block scarf until squared.

BACKING

Preshrink the silk fabric by hand-washing and then hanging to dry. Cut the fabric crosswise into two 9" x 45" (23cm x 114cm) strips. Sew the 2 strips together across 1 of the short ends to create a single 9" x 90" (23cm x 229cm) piece.
On a long work surface, lay the strip out with the wrong-side up. Lay the scarf right-side up on top of the fabric, being careful to keep it straight and squared. With the fabric marker, trace around the scarf. Remove scarf and cut fabric along traced outline.

Turn under ½" (13mm) along all edges of the fabric strip and press.

ASSEMBLING

Lay the knit scarf right-side down on the work surface. Lay the fabric backing on top with the finished side up. The backing will sit approximately ½" (13mm) in from the edge of the scarf all the way around. Carefully pin the fabric to the scarf at approximately 6" (15cm) intervals. With the sewing needle and thread, hand-stitch the backing to the knit scarf, making sure the stitches don't show on the right side of the scarf.

STITCH KEY

- ☐ Knit on RS, purl on WS
- ☒ Purl on RS, knit on WS
- ◩ K2tog
- ◪ P2tog
- ⊞ Cast on
- ✶ Bind off
- ◼ No Stitch

COLOR CHART

- ☐ Color A
- ▨ Color B
- ▦ Color C
- ◼ Color D

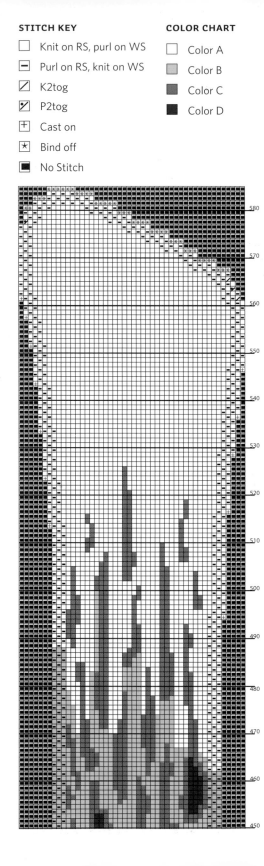

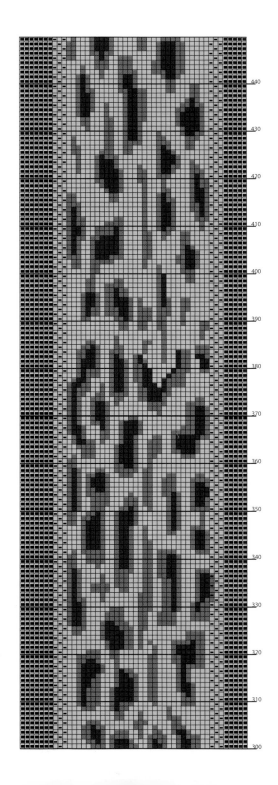

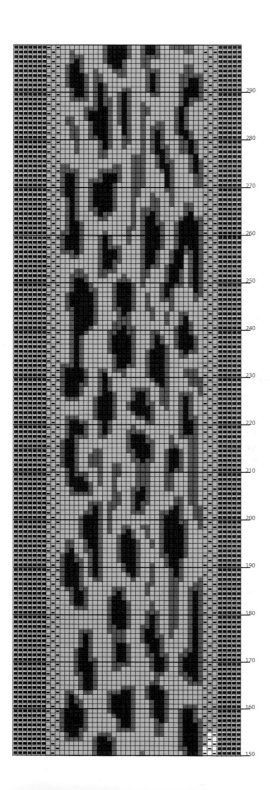

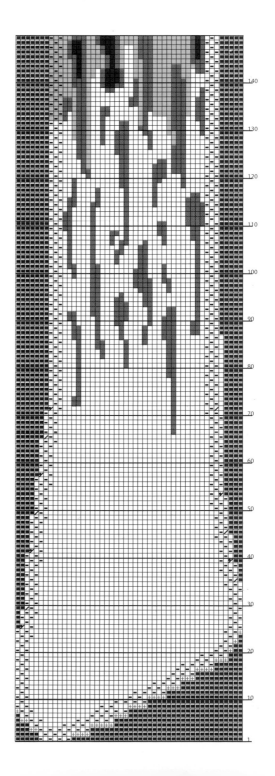

ARTIST TRADING CARDS

BEE SHAY

ALL CREATIVE PEOPLE NEED A MUSE, AND mixed-media artist Bee Shay wants to make sure they have one. That's why she hands out little "muse packets"—wrapped assortments of printed imagery, handmade papers, decorative pieces, and artist trading card blanks—to students or fellow artists at workshops and conferences. They're meant "to give inspiration," she says. Besides, sharing something handcrafted is very much a part of the world of artist trading cards, traded books, and other online exchanges, all of which have created a sense of community among far-flung collage and mixed-media enthusiasts, including Bee herself.

For the uninitiated, artist trading cards (ATCs) are baseball-card-size artworks, often illustrating some agreed-on theme and designed to be swapped, not sold. Used by Impressionist painters in the nineteenth century, their modern popularity can be traced to Swiss artist M. Vanci Stirnemann, who held trading sessions in 1996. Since then, the idea has spread, involving thousands of artists around the globe. Bee discovered the phenomenon in 2001 when someone handed her an ATC at a conference. She has gone on to show others how to craft ATCs, organized hundreds of exchanges, and

CLOCKWISE FROM TOP LEFT: Bee Shay crafting artist trading cards (ATCs); antique type blocks; an assortment of ATCs ; an inspirational studio array; Bee's handmade holder for ATCs.

had one of her cards chosen for a permanent exhibition at the Columbus Center for Paper & Book Arts. "For me the whole premise of ATCs resonates with how I teach," she says, "and how I am as a person."

Born in Bryn Mawr, Pennsylvania, Bee won a scholarship to an art college in Florida, though marriage and the first of three children intervened before she finished her degree. Back in Pennsylvania, she took workshops and ran her own art stenciling company, until, in 1994, a divorce prompted her to take a break. Two years later, "when I decided to get creative again, I discovered collage and mixed media." Inspired by an online article about visual and art

Artists choose a theme and create a work that circulates through the group.

journaling, she began looking for images to use, a search that led her to a nearby art store with a line of distinctive rubber stamps. Within a couple of months she was teaching regularly at the shop: "mixed-media classes, collage, rubber stamping."

By 2004, Bee was also participating in the burgeoning world of online exchanges, such as round robins in which half a dozen artists choose a theme and create a work that circulates

In her light-filled barn turned workspace Bee weighs some artistic options. Opposite: Her handmade book is an engaging mixed-media page-turner

through the group and makes its way back to its originator. "Or everyone does five pieces and sends them to a 'hostess,'" she explains. At the end, "everyone receives five back. That's the premise of ATCs."

Why the fascination with artist trading cards? "I thought it was a great way to study technique," she says, as well as to bolster a sense of community. "I was reaching out to people who were kindred spirits."

There are only a few rules for ATCs. Dimensions must be 2 ½ x 3 ½ inches (6.5cm x 9cm). And they are not to be sold or purchased. Any material is acceptable, but the back of the card should list the artist's contact information. "That way," Bee says, "if you want to know how someone did something, you can

find out. I've had an opportunity to interact with people all over the world."

Today Bee, who remarried in 2005, divides her time between Nantucket and an atmospheric home outside Philadelphia. Her husband, Lowell, is a thirty-year carpenter-turned-builder, and his own artistry is evident in their surroundings.

The house was built in 1852, she notes, while the barn—now her studio—was on the land perhaps fifty years earlier. Lowell transformed the space, using salvaged materials. "Almost one whole wall is glass," she says. "It's a wonderful place to work, and the students love it."

In fact, the place is an environmental muse packet, with printer's cases filled with type and papers, jars of buttons and brushes, bowls of sea creatures and other treasures from nature.

"Sometimes I photograph them and use the images in my work," Bee says.

She recently published a new book called *Collage Lab* and maintains a companion blog, but teaching creative methods keeps her energized, she insists, especially at the three-day Artfest in Port Townsend, Washington, where not long ago 125 of the 400 attendees participated in an ATC exchange. "I have each person make thirty cards," Bee says, using the overall Artfest theme. "They all get thirty back, but not necessarily their own."

She adds, "Someday I'd like to do a series of ATCs and leave them where they might be found. I'd put instructions on the back: 'If you want, make one and send it to me.' That way I'd find out what happened to the card. It would be interesting to see where they went."

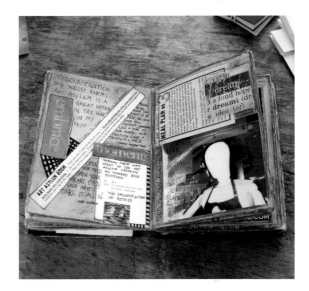

SERENDIPITY ARTIST TRADING CARD

DESIGNED BY Bee Shay **SKILL LEVEL** Easy

Bee Shay combines inspiration with the element of chance by painting on a single sheet of paper that will eventually produce eight ATCs. To each you add a personal image to create a focal point that states something about you.

MATERIALS (ENOUGH FOR 8 CARDS)

Gesso ink(s)

10" x 7" (25.5cm x 18cm) sheet of watercolor paper

Sea salt or kosher salt (large granules)

Torn, recycled papers, such as old maps, wrapping paper, newspaper, phone book pages, or magazine pages (All work well.)

Matte medium

Black magic marker, ink pad, gold leaf pen, or whatever marking instrument you like

8 images—copies or originals—in color or black and white (You will use these images as a focal point for each ATC. They should be no larger than 1½" x 2½" [3.8cm x 6.5cm].)

TOOLS

1" (2.5cm) chip brush

1" (2.5cm) flat brush

Small (size 0 or 1) detail brush

Small spray bottles: one for each color of ink you wish to uše

Sketch and wash pencil

Scissors or X-acto knife and cutting surface (such as a self-healing mat)

1. Using the chip brush, brush the gesso lightly onto the surface of the watercolor paper using irregular, uneven strokes. Let dry. Cover only about 20 percent of the surface of the watercolor paper.

2. Pour a small amount of ink into a spray bottle and add water to dilute. The solution should be about 30:70 ink to water. More ink will yield a stronger color. Start light, and if the resulting color is not deep enough, add more ink. You can always re-spray to get stronger colors.

3. Spray the watercolor paper with ink color(s) of your choice. Keep it simple: Three will work but so will one color. Let dry. Optionally, sprinkle the still-wet watercolor paper lightly with the salt, which creates small bursts of color. This works well when using one color or multiple colors.

4. Tear the recycled paper into small pieces, approximately 1" (2.5cm) or smaller.

5. Using the 1" (2.5cm) flat brush, coat the surface of the watercolor paper with a thin layer of matte medium. While still wet, begin to apply, at random, the small bits of recycled papers. To keep the composition consistent, use the same kind of recycled paper throughout.

6. When you're finished, coat the entire surface evenly with a thin coat of matte medium, and allow it to dry fully.

7. When the paper is dry, and satisfactory results have been obtained, turn it over, and cut it into eight pieces that measure 2½" x 3½" (6.5cm x 9cm). Turning it over will keep the eye from "choosing" where to cut. This method is about the process itself, not about controlling the process.

8. This is where the fun really begins. Turn the pieces over and position the focal point imagery. If they are not cut out already, then do so. It is much easier to work with a composition if the images are cut out and ready to use. Choose an image to be the focal point of each card. The key is to "keep it simple." This is a small area. If too much is going on, it will overwhelm the viewer and ruin the effect.

9. Once you are pleased with the design, glue the pieces using the matte medium with the 1" (2.5cm) flat brush to stick the focal points in place. Coat the entire surface again lightly to protect the image.

10. At this point the composition could be finished, but personally, the part I enjoy the most is when the almost-finished pieces are laid out, and can be played with and taken to another level. Using a sketch-and-wash pencil, outline the focal point lightly. Using a small detail brush and water, lightly go over the pencil lines to bleed them out, and away from the images for the purposes of shading. This will make the focal point really "pop."

11. The finished edge is always a nice final detail. Using a black magic marker, ink pad, gold leaf pen, or whatever marking instrument you like, run it along the cut edge on all four sides. This creates a frame of sorts around the piece. While subtle, it helps capture and define the small collage visually as it's held in a hand or laid on a surface.

12. Don't forget to sign the back with your contact information. Someone who receives the ATC may wish to ask you questions about how you did something. This way she can get in touch with you.

13. The Serendipity ATC is now ready for trading.

OPTIONS: Coat your finished ATC with beeswax. Or, for a shiny surface, use clear, thick, embossing medium or gloss matte medium. Use a gilding pen on the edges to add gold or silver touches. Affix tiny bits of gold or silver leaf to the surface before sealing to add shimmer. There are many other "embellishments" you could use. Raid your art stashes and just play with results.

D.I.Y. Become an Ambassador of Handmade

Mark Frauenfelder, editor of *Make* magazine and author of *Made by Hand,* has become a prominent advocate for the DIY lifestyle, one that goes beyond craft to take in all aspects of life. "One of the best things about craft is connecting with other people," he says. Here are his comments on why to become an "ambassador of handmade" . . . and tips on how to do it.

- The biggest benefit of making things ourselves is the connection with the community of makers. Human relations and friendship are valuable; the connection transcends religion and politics.

- Making means you have more control of your environment. Begin to notice and value the materials around you. You'll see their context, compared to the creations of the mass market.

- Start with activities that have bang for the buck, that have an impact. For me that's food-related,

but I'm also into practical crafts, like clothing or furnishings—things you use that have decorative elements, like knitting, crocheting, or crafting pottery.

- Spread the word that making gives you rewards and fulfillment you can't get any other way. You can't buy it; you can't stumble on it. The only way is by making something, and once you have a sense of ownership and that experience, you'll get the point.

KNITTING IS POLITICAL

LISA ANNE AUERBACH

IF YOU KNOCK ON THE DOOR OF LISA ANNE Auerbach's Los Angeles home—a lovingly renovated 1906 Craftsman bungalow she shares with her art historian husband, Louis Marchesano, and a couple of cats—she's likely to greet you wearing one of her sweaters, a moss green one, perhaps, from 2005, with the tongue-in-cheek statement "Everything I touch turns to Gold" and added fillips of "Bling, Bling, Kaching." The piece of knitwear is just one of a hundred she has made since 2004. Far more than garments (though they're eminently wearable), Lisa Anne's sweaters are personal billboards, proclaiming her views on subjects that range from politics and religion to art, work, and even the late pop icon Michael Jackson.

To say that they're conversation starters is both an understatement and also very much the point. They're meant to provoke a discussion. Sweaters are "different ways to put ideas in the world," says Lisa Anne, who also teaches at Pomona College and creates art installations as well as her intricately designed pullovers. Yet she never knitted a stitch until she finished graduate school. She grew up in one of the Chicago suburbs, got a BFA from Rochester Institute of Technology, and added an MFA from the Art Center College of Design in Pasadena. When she graduated out of her darkroom privileges, she deliberately turned to sweaters as an art form, teaching herself to knit from a library book and producing a lopi-style sweater with her initials charted into the hood as her first creation.

> To say they're conversation starters is both an understatement and also very much the point.

Inspired by the retro-patterned and -printed sweaters worn by Rick Nielsen, the guitarist of Cheap Trick, Lisa Anne set out to combine traditional and updated motifs with comments on issues that interested her.

"The sweaters function as vehicles for language," she says, adding, "It's about text and what it's like to be clothed by an idea. I liked a sweater as opposed to a T-shirt. It has more gravity; it lasts longer. It's worn outside, and it's part of the fabric, instead of put on." And when used in this way, the medium of knitting both changes and accentuates what each sweater says.

CLOCKWISE FROM TOP LEFT: Lisa Anne Auerbach starts a sharrow cardi; Lisa Anne in her studio; playful doorsill graffiti; the artist in LA on two wheels; a knit reminder of the Luddite Revolution.

Lisa Anne (times seven) appears in a photomural showing all the sweaters she created for *Take This Knitting Machine and Shove It*.

She produces her designs using Photoshop, layering background patterns with artful but often acerbic comments, and coming up with a chart that she fits onto a basic sweater shape. "I know where the front and back will be, and where the armholes are. I'm not a pattern designer," she insists. And though her first works were knitted by hand, she later bought two 180-needle, double-bed knitting machines and installed them in a studio at the side of her compact but productive fruit and vegetable garden. The machines now allow her to work more quickly and, as far as political issues are concerned, to be more timely. "The sweaters are a thing of the moment," she says, "and the machines save time."

For the Aspen Art Museum in 2008, she produced a series of red, white, and blue sweaters that spotlighted campaign slogans and candidates from each presidential election since 1800. Making different sweaters in different sizes, she allowed the sweaters to be "checked out" by museumgoers and worn around town. The goal was to foster a political dialogue.

Lisa Anne also expects something similar to happen when she wears her sweaters while riding one of her three bicycles. As a frequent bike commuter and bicycle activist in a city known more for its automobiles, she has designed pieces with a "share-the-road" theme as well as a rueful "I'm part of the problem" version, now that she also commutes by car.

Her work has attracted international attention, too. When England's Nottingham Contemporary museum commissioned her to do an installation in 2009, her show, titled *Take This Knitting Machine and Shove It*, highlighted sweaters and matching skirts hearkening back to the Luddite Revolution there, when workers smashed their machines. "We are all Heroes. We are all Terrorists," reads one top—which she created in Robin Hood green, of course.

While she was in Nottingham, she also organized something she called the Blanket of Ideas. "We did a knitting circle," she says, with twenty or thirty local knitters. Each of them made a square, roughly the same size, about some issue they were interested in. Afterward, Lisa Anne pieced the contributions together. But rather than neatly squaring it all off, she left open spaces at the bottom, so that it looks like more statements are still to come, in what could be seen as a never-ending dialogue.

D.I.Y. Writing with Yarn

Clara Parkes, author of *The Knitter's Book of Yarn*, lets you in on the secrets of choosing just the right fiber to express your sentiment in stitches:

- Envision your yarn as the nib of the pen. The fuzzier it is, the blurrier the letters. The more smooth and rounded the yarn, the clearer the letters. Because you're simultaneously writing the letters *and* creating the paper on which they are written, your stitches need to be distinct but also produce a cohesive fabric.

- Try a simple three- or four-ply yarn made from a soft and pliant wool or wool blend—the felt-tip pen of yarns. Some light fuzz on the yarn's surface helps fill in the fabric while still keeping your letters clear and legible.

  The greater the halo, the more subdued the letters. The smoother and more worsted-spun the yarn, the brighter and clearer those letters will be—but the more precise your tension will need to be, since there's less fuzz to fill in any inconsistencies.

- Two-ply yarns can render lettering rather like a calligraphy pen, with the visible ply structure adding a hint of shadowy wobble to the stitches and letters. The looser the angle of the ply, the less of a wobble you'll see; the tighter and springier the ply, the more those letters will take on the flickering shadows of the yarn.

- You can even use singles (one continual strand of twisted fiber) to achieve a relatively flat, one-dimensional effect. Be aware that you may see the contrasting colors being stranded behind your work. This is because singles lack the volume and three-dimensional body of three- or more ply yarns.

SHARROW CARDI

DESIGNED BY Lisa Anne Auerbach and Dorothy Orzel   **SKILL LEVEL** Experienced

Lisa Anne Auerbach has won acclaim for her politically charged knitted art. Though she doesn't normally produce patterns for apparel, she took this opportunity to promote one of her passions: urban biking. She came up with the overall look, designed the graphics, which incorporate a sharrow (the arrow symbol that indicates a shared bike/car lane), and worked with Dorothy Orzel to create this contemporary cardigan.

SIZE
XS (S, M, L, XL)

FINISHED MEASUREMENTS
Bust: 33 (36, 40, 44, 48)" (84 [91, 101.5, 112, 122]cm)

MATERIALS
5 (6, 6, 7, 8) skeins Brown Sheep Naturespun Sport, 100% wool, 1¾ oz (50g), 184 yd (168m) in Red Fox (A)

1 (1, 1, 1, 1) skeins Brown Sheep Naturespun Sport, 100% wool, 1¾ oz (50g), 184 yd (168m) in Pepper (B)

1 (1, 1, 1, 1) skeins Brown Sheep Naturespun Sport, 100% wool, 1¾ oz (50g), 184 yd (168m) in Goldenrod (C)

6 buttons ⅞" (2.2cm) in diameter

TOOLS
Size U.S. 4 (3.5mm) needles, or one size smaller than size used to obtain gauge

Size U.S. 5 (3.75mm) needles, or size to obtain gauge

Stitch markers

GAUGE
24 stitches and 28 rows = 4" (10cm) in stockinette stitch on larger needles

NOTE: To avoid a stair-step effect when doing bind-offs, slip the first stitch instead of working in pattern.

BACK

With smaller-size needles and B, cast on 98 (108, 120, 132, 144) stitches.

Work 8 rows in garter stitch.

Switch to larger needles.

Work 40 rows of the lower back chart in stockinette stitch.

With A, work 10 (12, 14, 16, 18) rows in stockinette stitch, ending with a WS row.

UPPER BACK

Next row K33 (38, 44, 50, 56), place marker, work 32 stitches of the upper back chart, place marker, k to end. Continue in stockinette stitch, slipping markers and working the chart until piece measures 12½ (12¾, 13, 13¾, 14½)" (32 [32.5, 33, 35, 37]cm) from the cast-on edge, ending with a WS row.

BEGIN ARMHOLE SHAPING

Continuing in stockinette stitch and chart pattern, bind off 7 (9, 11, 14, 17) stitches at the beginning of the next 2 rows—84 (90, 98, 104, 110) stitches

DECREASE ROW: K2, ssk, k to last 4 stitches, k2tog, k2.

Repeat decrease row on every RS row 26 (27, 29, 30, 32) more times—30 (34, 38, 42, 44) stitches.

Purl 1 row.

Bind off all stitches.

LEFT FRONT

With smaller-size needles and B, cast on 49 (54, 60, 66, 72) stitches.

Work 8 rows in garter stitch.

Switch to larger needles.

Work 40 rows of left front chart in stockinette stitch.

Continue working in stockinette stitch with A until piece measures 12½ (12¾, 13, 13¾, 14½)" (32 [32.5, 33, 35, 37]cm) from the cast-on edge, ending with a WS row.

BEGIN ARMHOLE SHAPING

ROW 1 (RS): Bind off 7 (9, 11, 14, 17) stitches, knit to end—42 (45, 49, 52, 55) stitches.

ROW 2: Purl.

ROW 3 (DECREASE ROW): K2, ssk, knit to end. Repeat decrease row every RS row 26 (27, 29, 30, 32) more times.

Purl next row.

At the same time, begin neck shaping.

When there are 25 (25, 27, 28, 30) stitches, ending with a RS row, bind off 4 (8, 10, 13, 13) stitches, and work to end.

Then bind off 1 stitch at the beginning of every WS row 10 (8, 8, 7, 8) times. Continue working decreases as established until 2 stitches remain, ssk. Fasten off by breaking yarn and pulling it through the last stitch.

RIGHT FRONT

With smaller-size needles and B, cast on 49 (54, 60, 66, 72) stitches.

Work 8 rows in garter stitch.

Switch to larger needles.

Work 40 rows of right front chart in stockinette stitch.

Continue working in stockinette stitch with A until piece measures 12½ (12¾, 13, 13¾, 14½)" (32 [32.5, 33, 35, 37]cm) from the cast-on edge, ending with a WS row.

BEGIN ARMHOLE SHAPING

ROW 1 (RS): Knit.

ROW 2: Bind off 7 (9, 11, 14, 17) stitches, purl to end—42 (45, 49, 52, 55) stitches.

ROW 3: Knit.

ROW 4 (DECREASE ROW): P2, ssp, purl to end. Repeat decrease row every WS row 26 (27, 29, 30, 32) more times.

At the same time, begin neck shaping.

When there are 25 (25, 27, 28, 30) stitches, ending with a WS row, bind off 4 (8, 10, 13, 13) stitches, and work to end.

Then bind off 1 stitch at the beginning of every RS row 10 (8, 8, 7, 8) times. Continue working decreases as established until 2 stitches remain, ssk. Fasten off by breaking yarn and pulling it through the last stitch.

LEFT SLEEVE

With smaller-size needles and B, cast on 52 (58, 60, 64, 68) stitches.

Work 8 rows in garter stitch.

Switch to larger needles.

Work 21 rows of Left Sleeve chart in stockinette stitch, working increase rows as follows:

Next row (RS increase row): K2, m1, knit to last 2 stitches, m1, k2.

Continuing in stockinette stitch with A, repeat increase row every 10 rows) 9 (8, 5, 3, 1) more times, every 6 rows 0 (2, 8, 5, 5) more times, then every 4 rows 0 (0, 0, 10, 16) more

times—76 (84, 92, 106, 118) stitches. Work in stockinette stitch without shaping until piece measures 17 (17 ½, 18, 18 ½, 19)" (43 [44.5, 45.5, 47, 48.5]cm), ending with a WS row.

SLEEVE CAP SHAPING

Bind off 7 (9, 11, 14, 17) stitches at the beginning of the next two rows—62 (66, 70, 78, 84) stitches.

Work 2 rows in stockinette stitch.

Decrease row (RS): K2, ssk, knit to last 4 stitches, k2tog, k2.

Repeat decrease row every 4 rows 3 (4, 5, 0, 0) more times, then every RS row 20 (19, 19, 29, 31) times—14 (18, 20, 20, 20) stitches. Bind off.

RIGHT SLEEVE

Work exactly as left sleeve, except work right sleeve chart.

FINISHING

Block all pieces.

BUTTON BAND

With right side facing, smaller needles and A, pick up 96 (100, 102, 108, 114) stitches along the left front edge. Work 8 rows in k1, p1 rib, ending with RS row. Bind off neatly in rib.

BUTTONHOLE BAND

With right side facing, smaller needles and A, pick up 96 (100, 102, 108, 114) stitches along the right front edge. Work 2 rows in k1, p1 rib, ending with RS row.

BUTTONHOLE ROW 1: Rib 6, *bind off the next 3 stitches, rib 17 (18, 18, 20, 21); repeat from * 3 more times, bind off next 3 stitches, rib to end.

BUTTONHOLE ROW 2: Work in rib pattern as established, casting on 3 stitches over each bind-off in previous row.

Work 4 more rows in rib pattern, ending with a RS row. Bind off neatly in rib.

Sew sleeves to fronts and back. Sew side and underarm seams, making sure underarm points of front and back are aligned.

ROLL COLLAR

With right side facing, smaller-size needles, and B, starting at center of Buttonhole band. Pick up 92 (104, 112, 120, 126) stitches evenly around the neck to center of Button band.

NOTE: When the sweater is buttoned, the collar will meet at center front, but not overlap.

Starting with a purl row, work 8 rows in stockinette stitch, then bind off all stitches loosely.

Weave in ends.

Sew buttons on Button band, positioning them opposite the buttonholes.

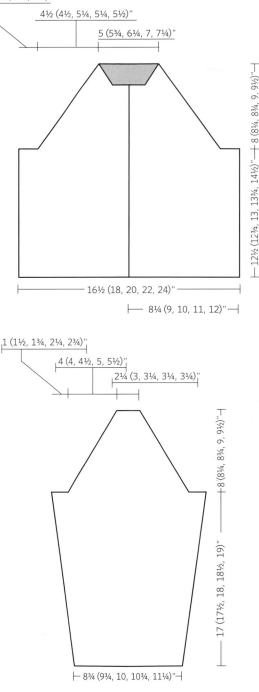

UPPER BACK CHART

67
65
63
61
59
57
55
53
51
49
47
45
43
41
39
37
35
33
31
29
27
25
23
21
19
17
15
13
11
9
7
5
3
1

- ■ Color A
- ■ Color B
- □ Color C

LOWER BACK CHART

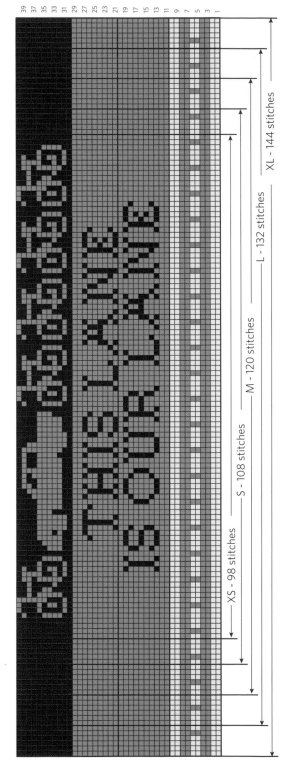

39 37 35 33 31 29 27 25 23 21 19 17 15 13 11 9 7 5 3 1

XL - 144 stitches

L - 132 stitches

M - 120 stitches

S - 108 stitches

XS - 98 stitches

LEFT FRONT CHART

39
37
35
33
31
29
27
25
23
21
19
17
15
13
11
9
7
5
3
1

← XS - 49 stitches →
← S - 54 stitches →
← M - 60 stitches →
← L - 66 stitches →
← XL - 72 stitches →

RIGHT FRONT CHART

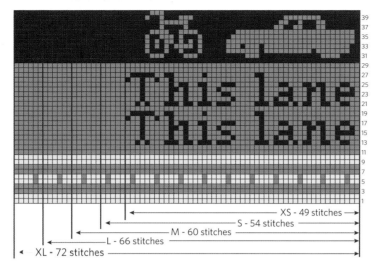

39
37
35
33
31
29
27
25
23
21
19
17
15
13
11
9
7
5
3
1

XS - 49 stitches
S - 54 stitches
M - 60 stitches
L - 66 stitches
XL - 72 stitches

LEFT SLEEVE CHART

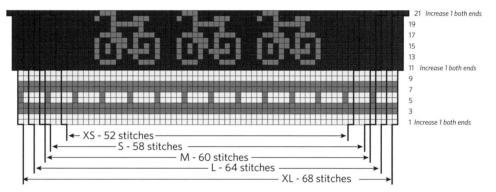

21 *Increase 1 both ends*
19
17
15
13
11 *Increase 1 both ends*
9
7
5
3
1 *Increase 1 both ends*

XS - 52 stitches
S - 58 stitches
M - 60 stitches
L - 64 stitches
XL - 68 stitches

RIGHT SLEEVE CHART

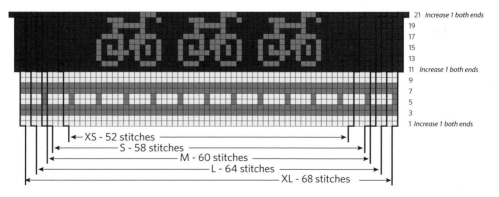

21 *Increase 1 both ends*
19
17
15
13
11 *Increase 1 both ends*
9
7
5
3
1 *Increase 1 both ends*

XS - 52 stitches
S - 58 stitches
M - 60 stitches
L - 64 stitches
XL - 68 stitches

NOTE: This is the number of stitches on the needle as you end the garter stitch border. You will immediately increase 1 stitch on both ends as you begin working chart (as diagrammed).

PART II
RECRAFTING

They say everything old will be new again, and certainly that's been true in the craft world, where traditional women's arts have enjoyed a resurgence of popularity. As knitting, crocheting, sewing, and embroidery have found new fans, however, they have also been tweaked, adapted, and refashioned for the times.

That's especially evident when it comes to sensibility. Where women used to gather, needles in hand, for a bit of genteel gossip, now we come to "stitch 'n bitch," thanks to the encouragement of Debbie Stoller, groundbreaking editor of *Bust* magazine. She brought a new forthright vocabulary to her own *Stitch 'n Bitch* books and helped give birth to the knit and crochet groups we participate in at local yarn stores across the country. At the same time, embroiderers and quilters have updated their designs, replacing cutesy with retro and cuddly with "in your face." In the nicest possible way, of course.

The crocheters among us have rediscovered new possibilities for granny squares—yes, you can use them to create an iPad cover—and may use eco-chic organic yarns in an array of contemporary shades. Certainly they have come up with new crocheted motifs unlike anything Granny ever produced.

THE PAST

And while feminists a generation ago considered the humble apron a symbol of oppression, their daughters are out collecting vintage examples and sewing new ones without a second thought. If this is partly the result of changing styles, there's also a real desire to connect with the women in our past. Turning backward, we celebrate the work and life of relatives, friends, and neighbors, embrace it with new fervor, and make it relevant for the future.

NOT YOUR GRANDMOTHER'S EMBROIDERY

JENNY HART

THOUGH SHE'S RUN A BUSINESS CALLED Sublime Stitching for almost a decade, Jenny Hart can still remember the first time she really wanted to try embroidery. Around the year 2000, she was on an extended visit to the home she grew up in, near the Illinois-Iowa border. It was a difficult time emotionally, as she tried to deal with grief over a death in the family and to connect with her mother, who also was ill. Bored with television, Jenny thought of needlework. She knew that her mother had the materials and could show her what to do. But Jenny wasn't interested in outlining cutesy ducks. An accomplished artist, she chose to replicate a photo of her mother, circa 1952.

"I had no idea what to do," the then-novice embroiderer says. "I plunged the needle in from the front, and then realized, OK, now I know why you have to start from the back." After her mother demonstrated a split stitch, Jenny found the craft absorbing. She never looked back. Since then, she has produced embroidered portraits, hundreds of patterns, kits for beginners, and books and Web sites about embroidery. In the process she has irrevocably changed the image of the traditional craft.

Jenny had a solid art background, beginning with drawing classes as a five-year-old and

> ## "I hung up my guitar and started embroidering."

continuing with studies at the University of Kansas. After graduation, she worked at the Spencer Museum of Art and at the Blanton Museum in Austin, where she and her then-husband also performed with their garage band. But the spate of family illnesses took a toll on her. "I hung up my guitar and started embroidering," she says. "It was the first time I'd relaxed in years."

For her, the appeal of the craft lay in its bright stitching, its simplicity, and especially its textures. "You cannot do that with a pencil," she says. There was also the fact that you could see it was done by hand. Embroidery is "pure decoration, secondary to a functional object, like a tea towel, a cozy, or a pillowcase. I began to think, What if I used it as a medium for art?"

After that first illustration of her mother, she

CLOCKWISE FROM TOP LEFT: Jenny Hart favors a quiet corner for artistic pursuits; DIY down to the details; Jenny's talent is no mystery; a studio corner; a few examples of her collection of vintage embroidery.

Working in her home office, Jenny develops designs for Sublime Stitching. Opposite: Her creations range from simple statements (left) to complex portraits (right).

did portraits of other family members, and when she ran out of people to stitch, turned to pictures from the 1950s.

She showed the work to a gallery owner, whose enthusiasm led to a show. "All the embroidery sold out," Jenny remembers. "People wanted more." She obliged them with designs unlike those that anyone with an embroidery hoop and floss had ever seen. "I'd do vintage tattoos and pinups," she says. "The bar for what was out there was unusually low."

About this time she discovered that Tina Sparkles, who was then crafting custom cotton guitar straps, was another Austin resident. They arranged to meet, and Tina brought along

Jennifer Perkins, future founder of the Naughty Secretary Club. "Tina, Jennifer, and I were all bitten by the entrepreneurial bug," says Jenny, who was thinking about building a business based on her embroidery designs. "I wanted to create the company that I wished was there when I wanted to learn." With a $1,000 loan from her father, she launched Sublime Stitching, created a blog and Web site, and began turning out patterns based on her own aesthetic. "There was no Etsy then. It was the Wild Crafty West."

The women got together every month or two, bounced ideas off each other, shared the cost of an ad, and the Austin Craft Mafia was born. The informal group, which grew to nine members,

"traded promo cards and did cross-promotions," says Jenny. "Our businesses could work together; they weren't in competition." As the word spread, the ACM inspired similar groups in other cities. "The craft industry had no idea that there was a huge independent market," she says.

Her work also got a boost when *Bust* editor Debbie Stoller commissioned her to stitch an illustration of a young woman about to join the army after 9/11. "They generously listed my Web site along with my byline. It was the first thing that really drove traffic to my site."

The traffic has not slowed, and Jenny has not only turned out sheets of her own inimitable patterns but also has worked with concert poster illustrators to develop an artists' series. Since Sublime Stitching outgrew her garage, she's carved out an office at home. But she keeps a spare bedroom as a place to relax, watch TV, and create artwork, like the pencil portraits she drew of high school classmates for a gallery show. "I love the challenge of something I haven't tried yet," she says, adding that she also still loves embroidery. "It's keeping me sane."

CHAWNE KIMBER, who maintains a journal-like stream of photos on Flickr, started embroidering because she wanted to say more with her quilts, which was her first craft: "It's difficult to get text and images into a quilt using patchwork." Some of the subjects she took on, however, would have been shocking at our grandmothers' quilting bees.

Terminology for bowel movements, for example. "I did 'Pooh,' and it went downhill from there," she says. Another of Chawne's quilts-in-progress was inspired by an e-mail spam message that mentioned growing your love. An image of a banana took hold. Before long, she had used Twitter and Flickr to ask friends and acquaintances to send her suggestive instances of spam, which she has illustrated and stitched in thirty-six embroidered squares. "They're getting progressively more detailed."

The trend toward outspoken embroidery is rooted in several things, Chawne suggests. "We're younger than past generations, less mature. Grandmother wanted a quilt as a source of warmth, and only secondarily as a possible way of expressing herself. I don't have to conform to social standards, and I don't have to worry about the sensibility of a family member who might use it."

Tucson artist **PAUL NOSA** turned to embroidery half a dozen years ago as an outgrowth of his drawing, then brought it up-to-date by combining an interest in alternative energy with the traditional craft. "I wanted to make functional art," he says. He began to wonder if he "could draw with a sewing machine." Indeed he could.

At first he embroidered shirt-size abstract designs and then concentrated on patches ("mini-canvases"), producing free-flowing images of fanciful humans, animals, and bicycles. Nosa also designed a solar-powered sewing machine that he takes to makers' fairs, where, in an interactive spirit, he embroiders scenarios that visitors describe in five words or less.

HOT STUFF STITCHING

DESIGNED BY Jenny Hart   **SKILL LEVEL** Easy

Hot fun in the kitchen! Embroidering this motif onto tea towels or a finished apron is one of the simplest projects to take on and can easily be done in two evenings. Jenny stitched this pattern using only three colors: bright red, hazard orange, and a dark gray.

MATERIALS

Tea towel, cotton apron, or place mat

1 skein each of six-strand cotton embroidery floss in red, orange, and dark gray

TOOLS

Carbon transfer paper or transfer pen

Iron

7" (18cm) embroidery hoop (optional)

Basic, sharp needle

1. Copy or scan the "Hot Stuff" template, enlarging to your desired size. Depending on the transfer method you use (see step 2), decide if you need to reverse the lettering or not.

2. Transfer the pattern. There are numerous options for transferring a pattern onto fabric. Which method you use will determine if you need to reverse the image. I suggest one of these two methods:

Carbon transfer paper. If you are using carbon transfer paper, you will not need to reverse the image. Lay the carbon transfer paper over the area you want to stitch, and then lay the design on top, with the design appearing faceup. Secure the design in place so it won't shift, and trace. Be sure to work on a hard, smooth surface.

Transfer pen. When using a transfer pen, you will trace directly along the lines of the printed design and then lay it facedown against your fabric and use the sheet just like an iron-on. Because this design has lettering, it will need to be reversed if you plan to use this method.

3. Putting your fabric on the hoop (optional). Once the pattern is on your fabric, place your fabric on the embroidery hoop (if you'll be using one). Position the imprinted fabric over the nonadjustable hoop, place the adjustable hoop (the one with the screw) over it, and press down, stretching the fabric like a drumhead. Tighten the screw, gently pulling your fabric taut to make sure it is smooth and free of wrinkles. You are now officially ready to stitch. Almost.

4. Fire up that needle!
Pull a length of floss about 13" (33cm) long (approximately the length from your fingertips to your elbow). Six-strand embroidery floss is made up of six tiny strands that you can pull apart for finer detail, or use all six strands, as I did, for a chunkier look.

To make it even easier, the entire pattern was worked in a simple back stitch. Take a single stitch along your pattern line. Jump ahead (skip) a space along the pattern line with each new stitch, and bring your needle down into the endpoint of your last stitch, closing the gap. Boom! You have an awesome buffet showpiece. Be sure to invite over that cute fireman living next door.

A NEW TAKE ON OLD DOMESTIC ARTS

CATHERINE CLARK AND KATIE METZGER

WHEN CATHERINE CLARK AND KATIE METZGER moved the Brooklyn General Store to its present location a couple of years ago, they left traces of the shop's previous occupant. Both women had great affection for "Frank's Department Store: Name Brand Clothing. Always Something New," where they could buy underwear and find racks of vintage kids' clothing. And they wanted to preserve some ties to the traditional character of their Carroll Gardens neighborhood, where longtime Italian residents now mix with young, professional families.

So, outside, above the window display for their yarn-fabric-crafts emporium, you can still make out the old Frank's sign, and, inside, an old-fashioned ladder reaches a wall of shelves built in long ago. Their shop is a "community place," says Catherine, where crafters can connect with each other, find materials, or take sewing, knitting, or other classes in a supportive, comfortable environment. And if a former Frank's customer wanders in, well, that just underlines the welcoming feel of an old-time general store.

"We both loved the thought of Oleson's

CLOCKWISE FROM TOP LEFT: Brooklyn General Store adds whimsy to practicality; Katie Metzger (at left) and Catherine Clark at the sewing machine; a sign of the past; the proprietors and their wares.

Mercantile," from TV's *Little House on the Prairie,* she says, "and we wanted the same concept in our neighborhood. Brooklyn General has at its core a desire to bring people back to a time when we were more connected to the processes of life—cooking, sewing, knitting, building—making everyday necessities."

The two women have known each other since their oldest kids were in preschool a dozen or so years ago. But their crafting passions

The enterprise kicked off when she met a couple who had vintage fabrics for sale.

reach back far beyond that. Catherine learned to sew early and remembers helping her mother make headbands and Christmas ornaments for a holiday crafts fair. "When I was in high school, I had a teddy bear business. I set up shop in the basement of my parents' house and sewed nonstop. I made 150 bears and sold them on the street at Christmas." She majored in art and worked as an assistant for several sculptors in New York City, until she became a nurse-midwife, a practice she still maintains.

Marcie Farwell, who teaches sewing classes at Brooklyn General Store, turns yarn into casual adornment. Opposite: the raw materials of knit fashion.

"Midwifery is more of an art than a science," she says. "And midwifery and Brooklyn General have to do with women and community and sharing information."

Katie grew up outside Washington, D.C., where her mother, an artist, always had art supplies in her studio. After college, Katie taught kindergarten in New York City. "I liked to do art projects," she remembers. "I'd get the kids to make a quilt; each kid would make a bug or a flower with a little bit of sewing, and I'd piece them together." While in graduate school, she and a friend would sew dresses and sell them on the street. "They were simple shifts," she says. "We called ourselves Crooked Stitches." Later, after her son was born, she began sewing baby outfits labeled "Fruity Suits." "There's instant

gratification with sewing," she notes. "It's what makes me happy."

Brooklyn General got its start in January 2003, in the basement of Catherine's brownstone, across the street from Frank's. She ordered $1,000 worth of yarn, put up a sign, and opened the door. But the enterprise really kicked off when she attended a flea market and met a couple who had vintage fabrics for sale.

"We walked into the warehouse," Katie says, "and there was fabric from the forties and fifties, still on the bolt and in good condition. Florals and prints. Not like fabric you see in stores today. Every pattern was beautiful, and there it was in a dusty warehouse, the biggest treasure you ever imagined." They bought it all.

After that, they added other hard-to-find

supplies: wool-felt fabric that they got from a company in Holland. Magic Cabin doll-making supplies. Milk paint. Embroidery hoops and thread. The shop had the feel of a "cozy nest" that surrounded you with warm colors and fibers. "People would hang out and talk about what they wanted to do," says Katie. But sometimes cozy turned into crowded. So when Frank's Department Store posted its "Going Out of Business" notice, they made the move.

There's still a comfortable couch for customers to hang out on, and an open invitation to Friday morning breakfasts. There's room for enough machines to hold sewing classes. And time to think about other projects to take on, like "a school of crafts where you could do cooking or woodworking and have space for a gallery to show people's work," Katie adds.

"Katie and I also wanted to come up with a simple wardrobe for women," says Catherine. "A housedress fits into that concept. You throw it on, it looks good, and you're good to go."

Share Your Passion by Teaching

Mothers and grandmothers may have been our traditional craft teachers, but these days we should all learn to pass along tips and techniques. By teaching, crafters can learn more about their own work, says **Shannon Okey**, author of *The Knitgrrl Guide to Professional Knitwear Design* and other books. "It helps me find better ways to do what I do," she notes, "which then trickles back into my teaching—a sort of endless loop." She shares some tips on making the switch from maker to teacher.

- Start by volunteering at your local yarn or craft store, so that when someone needs a technique explained or demonstrated, you're the go-to person. It's a nonthreatening environment in which to get started.

- Don't be afraid of online teaching. Opening up skills acquisition to a broader audience is crucial to engaging people and keeping them interested. Not everyone has a local yarn or craft store or can travel to a fiber arts festival or craft fair. Plus, online classes may be less intimidating when it comes to posting a question.

- Remember that students are there because they want to learn what you have to teach.

- Be open to new experiences and information during class. No one knows all the answers, and if you respect each other's needs and make the actual learning fun, everyone (including you) will have a good time.

BELLA BROOKLYN HOUSEDRESS

DESIGNED BY Catherine Clark and Katie Metzger   **SKILL LEVEL** Intermediate

At Brooklyn General, the older Italian women of the neighborhood still come in looking for the housedresses sold by the previous shop—dresses they would wear all day long. This updated version takes the housedress out of the house and, unlike the tentlike garments evokes earlier styles that were classy while remaining simple and easy to wear.

SIZE
S (M, L)

FINISHED MEASUREMENTS
Bust: 35 (37, 40)" (89 [94, 101.5]cm)

MATERIALS
2 yd (183cm) 1" (2.5cm) gridded pattern paper or gridded interfacing, such as Tru-Grid Graph Material
2 yd (183cm) of 44/45" (112/114cm) lightweight, woven fabric, such as a quilt print
⅝ yd (57cm) of any width lightweight, fusible interfacing
20" (51cm) regular dress zipper
Thread to match, or contrast with, your fabric

TOOLS
Pencil
Scissors
Sewing pins
Sewing machine
Sewing needle

SEAM ALLOWANCE
⅝" (16mm)

NOTE: Make the Bella Brooklyn Housedress work for you by tinkering with the pattern template—for instance, adding sleeves and swapping buttons for the front zipper, as in the green-print version opposite.

1. Prewash fabric according to manufacturer's instructions.

2. Draft the pattern. Scale up your desired size and version of the pattern to 1" (2.5cm) gridded paper or interfacing. One square on the diagram will equal one square on your paper. Be sure to transfer grain lines, notches, and other markings.

3. Cut your pattern pieces. Fold the fabric in half, right side to right side. Lay out the pattern pieces on the fabric. Make sure all pattern pieces that say "Cut on fold" are placed on the fold. Cut the pieces out carefully.

4. Preassembly. Fuse interfacings to the wrong side of facings, following manufacturer's instructions.

5. Sew Front and Back Neck Facings at the shoulder line, right side to right side. Finish outside edge.

NOTE: Seams can be finished by serging, zigzag, or turning under ¼" (6mm) and edge stitching.

6. Make the Pocket. Finish top edge of Pocket. Turn back at fold line and press. Align Pocket with notches on Side Fronts. Stay stitch to Side Front at ¼" (13mm).

7. Sew Side Fronts to Fronts, right side to right side, matching notches. Finish seams.

8. Sew Center Fronts together, right side to right side, from hem to circle mark. Back stitch. Install zipper following manufacturer's instructions. The top stop of the zipper should sit about 1" (2.5cm) below the raw edge of the neck. Finish the seam below the circle mark.

BELLA BROOKLYN HOUSEDRESS

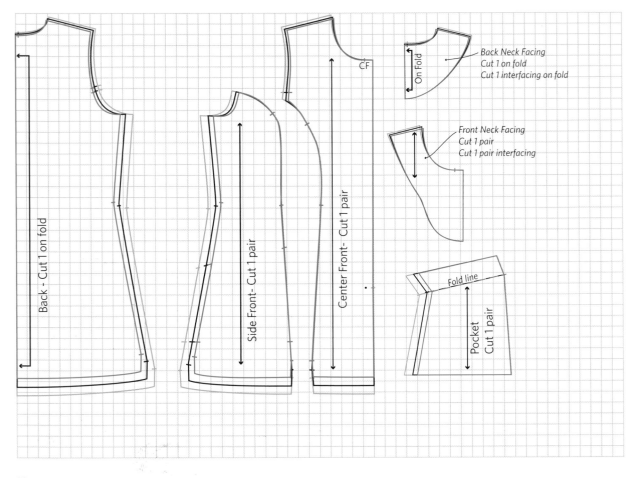

Back Neck Facing
Cut 1 on fold
Cut 1 interfacing on fold

On Fold

Front Neck Facing
Cut 1 pair
Cut 1 pair interfacing

Back - Cut 1 on fold

Side Front- Cut 1 pair

Center Front- Cut 1 pair

CF

Fold line

Pocket
Cut 1 pair

Key

— = Small

— = Medium

— = Large

Scale ☐ = 1"

⅝" Seam allowance included on all patterns

9. Sew Fronts to Back at shoulder seam, right side to right side. Finish seams.

10. Sew Fronts to Back at side seams, right side to right side. Finish seams.

11. Attach Neck Facing: Fold back ¼" (6mm) along front edges of Neck Facing and press. Pin Neck Facing to garment neck, right side to right side. Sew, neatly angling zipper tape ends out of the way at Center Front. Trim seam allowance to ¼"(6mm). Turn the facing to the correct side and press. With needle and thread, secure the facing to the garment by making a few stitches at zipper edges and shoulder seam allowances.

12. Armhole: Stay stitch the armhole at ⅝" (16mm). Trim seam to ¼" (6mm). Serge or zigzag edge. Carefully press armhole, turning the raw edge to the inside and rolling the stay-stitched line just to the inside. Topstitch armhole at ³⁄₁₆" (5mm), just catching the finished edge.

13. Hem: Finish raw edge. Turn up 1½" (3.8cm) and press. Topstitch at 1¼" (3cm).

LOS ANGELES CONSERVANCY
SEP California CA 2010
V 7704546
CROCHET
I BRAKE FOR HISTORIC LANDMARKS!

RETURN OF THE GRANNY SQUARE

ELLEN BLOOM

ON ANY GIVEN THURSDAY EVENING, YOU'RE likely to find Ellen Bloom upstairs at the Original Farmers Market in the heart of Los Angeles, a granny square in her hand, together with a dozen or more knitters and crocheters. The enthusiastic Stitch 'n Bitch group, one of six or seven in Los Angeles, has been meeting here since 2004, and for Ellen the location is a congenial mash-up of her background and interests. The Farmers Market is as much an LA institution as the Hollywood sign, and the native Angeleno is as passionate about the city's architecture, its art and popular culture, and its inimitable style as she is about crocheted motifs.

"The Farmers Market is the vortex of Los Angeles," she says. "Everyone gets pulled into it eventually." And it's especially nice for the SnB, since there's wine and food available for the wide range of participants. "We've got girls twenty-two and women sixty. Guys come, too." On special occasions, like the costume-required Halloween Stitch 'n Witch or the periodic stash swaps,

as many as thirty yarnies may show up. The gatherings are often recorded by Ellen's husband, professional photographer Larry Underhill.

Ellen attributes her love of Los Angeles style to her parents' appreciation of the 1950s aesthetic. As for crafts, "My mother knitted, and my grandmother crocheted. But I learned to knit at seven, when I was in the Brownies. I think the troop leader taught us to get us quiet. We made little squares."

In those days the city was rich with yarn

When crochet became popular in the early 1970s, she consulted a book and taught herself to make granny squares.

stores, including one where the proprietor would measure her customers for custom knitwear patterns. Ellen crafted her own versions, notably dirndl skirts for her Barbie dolls, which she is happy to pull out from an original case, along with miniature accessories that include eyeglasses and a tiny stole from an aunt's refashioned mink. "I get all my ideas about accessorizing from Barbie," jokes Ellen.

CLOCKWISE FROM TOP LEFT: Ellen Bloom's crochet creations draw on So-Cal mosaics for colorful inspiration; friends come to craft; auto-definition; retro motif meets high tech; Ellen shows off the versatile granny square.

"I kept knitting through high school," she remembers, and when crochet became popular in the early 1970s, she consulted a book and taught herself to make granny squares. "It was much faster than knitting, and I'm impatient!"

She was still at it years later, when she put a longstanding interest in music to work by booking blues artists. By the late 1980s she was in radio, first operating the sound board on a Roots music show and then—as LA Ell—sharing the microphone with harmonica virtuoso John Juke Logan on the *Friday Night Blues Revue.* "I'd get on the radio and knit or crochet," she remembers. The show stayed on the air for eight years, until the station went all-talk, and Ellen hung up her headphones for good. Long before that happened, though, she'd met Larry, another Angeleno on a music-oriented vacation.

"We feed each other's habits," she says. Along with their appreciation of alternative music, the two are active in the Modern Committee of the LA Conservancy, which preserves historic buildings in the city. The walls of their 1928 cottage are hung with bright, richly textured paintings—some by Ellen, some by other local artists—that highlight the diversity of Los Angeles' neighborhoods.

And then there are the collections: rows of tiki mugs, statues, and masks; musical instruments; records; three impressive old cars (a '65 Falcon Ranchero, a '55 Chevy Bel-Air, and a '63 Dodge Dart); pottery by fifties designer

How to Organize a Craft Night

Tired of making something by yourself or perhaps with one other friend? It's probably time to organize a craft night—a great way to glean new information, techniques, and inspiration, says **Amy Singer**, founder and editor of **Knitty.com**. But how do you actually round up like-minded makers and keep them motivated? Amy has a few tips:

- First you need a group. Start with friends, but then think bigger. Use social networking sites, like Ravelry or Twitter, and remember to blog that you're interested in starting something.

- Pick a location that's appropriate. Coffee shops have worked well for stitch 'n bitch, but probably won't suit quilters, who might prefer a private home with a big dining room table. Make sure the light level is appropriate to the craft.

- If you choose a public place, talk with the shop owner and get her buy-in. She will be glad to have you.

- When you publicize the craft night, make it sound established and ongoing. If it's a stitch 'n bitch, that's easy. Remember: If it's just one time, it's a party!

- Have prizes or a craft exchange. People like to win things. You can start with yarn from your stash, beads you've never used, or craft paper you've changed your mind about. We all love a takeaway.

- To keep it fresh, you need a leader, someone vaguely charismatic who's willing to take charge but who's also willing to listen to the creative ideas of others. Then get together and get inspired!

Sascha Brastoff; vintage brooches, necklaces, and poodle jewelry; and bins and bins of yarn. Best of all, considering the recent resurgence of granny square mania (some of which can be traced to Ellen herself), is an entire "granny square suite."

For her, the multicolored, crocheted squares have the appeal of a brilliant mosaic. "I love tile and the bright colors. Southern California is about brightness," Ellen points out. And she proselytizes for crochet, among other vintage topics, on her "LA Is My Beat" blog.

"Crochet is sculptural," she notes, and she's made use of that to create a crocheted camera, a taco, even an Oreo cookie. If pressed, Ellen admits that, yes, she could probably come up with a crocheted tiki, too. But for now she's set her sights on granny square upholstery, perhaps a cover for a chair or ottoman.

What's the appeal? It's cyclical, she says, "like any style. When I look at a pattern book, I think, I've seen that in the 1970s, but we change it to make it our own, with nicer materials and nicer colors." Granny squares will always have fans. "After all, they're the building blocks of fashion."

Makers Jam

KIM WERKER, the founder and blogger of Crochetme.com, notes one reason crocheters are more visible now is the Internet. "We're able to connect online with a massive community to fuel our inspiration, teach us new techniques, and support us." Support is key. "No one is going to make a snide comment about your being a thirty-year-old granny."

As for why crochet has been so cyclical, she points out that crochet "cannot be made by machine. When crochet goes out of fashion, it disappears from shelves. So we associate it with the iconic crochet fashions the last time it was popular. Today there's no particular iconic crocheted item. It's popular in fashion, in home décor, and toys."

What's in the future? "The yarn industry has started to accept crochet as a fashion craft," says Kim. "It's expected that a crocheted garment will have a pleasing fabric and a flattering fit. There's a lot of enthusiasm about lightweight yarns, drapey fabrics, and motifs."

Crochet's renewed cachet has also turned a spotlight on small, fantastic creations, like popular Japanese *amigurumi*. In Los Angeles, **REGINA RIOUX GONZALEZ** has been turning out odd vegetables (everything from zombie asparagus to killer corn), jellyfish, and, um, crocheted eyeballs. This is crochet as tiny contemporary sculpture, but sculptures that she helps others to replicate with her patterns. "If you do basic stitches," she says, "you can make an eyeball. Crochet comes in waves. "There's been a twenty-year break, but now it's back." Her projects are "organic or humorous." Witness her bacon slabs. "Growing up in California, I do yoga and eat mostly great stuff. But I like to be a provocateur. I love pop culture, and I try to use that."

GRANNY GREENBAG

DESIGNED BY Ellen Bloom   **SKILL LEVEL** Easy

Retro chic advocate Ellen Bloom has been preaching the gospel of granny squares in Los Angeles for years, living in her own casa de crochet and teaching the craft to countless others. Here she transforms a staple of modern life, the reusable market bag, by covering it with granny squares. If you prefer a look that's more New England beach than California colorful, try the pattern using cotton pastels.

FINISHED MEASUREMENTS

The bag, as shown, finishes at approximately 12 ½" wide x 18 ½" high x 6 ½" deep (32cm x 47cm x 16.5cm) and fits over a commercial grocery tote bag 12" wide x 18" high x 6" (30.5cm x 45.5cm x 15cm) deep.

You can use any size grocery tote. The size and number of granny motifs needed may vary, depending on the size of your tote.

The instructions below will produce a granny motif approximately 4" x 4" (10cm x 10cm). Generally, one crochet round on the motif is equal to one 1" (2.5cm). For a larger motif, add another round of crochet.

MATERIALS

2 skeins Brown Sheep Lambs Pride Worsted Weight Yarn, 85% Wool, 15% Mohair, 4 oz (113g), 190 yd (173m), in Christmas Green

¼ skein of each in Orange Creamsicle; Orange You Glad; Red Hot Passion; and Wild Mustard

Cascade 220 Superwash Wool Worsted Weight Yarn, 100% Superwash Wool, 3 ½ oz (100g), 220 yd (201m), ¼ skein of each in Lime, Medium Blue, Rust, Pink, Light Purple, Light Blue, and Aqua

Cascade 220 Wool Worsted Weight Yarn, 100% Peruvian highland wool, 3 ½ oz (100g), 220 yd (201m), ¼ skein of each in Hot Pink and Blue/Purple

Commercial grocery tote bag (cloth or plastic)

TOOLS

Size G-6 (4mm) crochet hook
Tapestry needle
Sewing needle and thread in main color
Sewing pins
Binder clips

NOTE: This Granny GreenBag uses many colors: two contrasting colors for the center of each motif, and the same color for the last round of each motif. The main color yarn is matched to the handles of a reusable tote bag.

GRANNY MOTIF

(MAKE 24 MOTIFS, OR AS NEEDED FOR YOUR SIZE BAG)

FOUNDATION ROUND: With one color, chain 5, join with a slip stitch to form a ring.

ROUND 1: Chain 3 (this counts as the first double crochet stitch), 11 double crochet in ring; join with a slip stitch in third chain of beginning chain-3. You will have 12 double crochet stitches.

ROUND 2: Slip stitch into the space between beginning chain-3 stitch and first double crochet. Chain 3, 1 double crochet in same space. *2 double crochet in next space. Repeat from * until you have 24 double crochet stitches. Join with a slip stitch in the third chain of the beginning chain-3. Fasten off.

ROUND 3: With a new color, join the yarn in any space. Chain 3, 2 double crochet in the same space, skip the next space. *3 double crochet in the next space, skip the next space; repeat from * until you have 36 stitches. Fasten off.

ROUND 4: With MC, join the yarn in any space between two 3-double crochet groups. Chain 3, (2 double crochet, chain 2, 3 double crochet) in the same space (corner made). [3 double crochet in the next space (as above)] twice, (3 double crochet, chain 2, 3 double crochet) in the next space; repeat from * twice, [3 double crochet in the next space] twice. Join with a slip stitch in the third chain of the beginning chain-3. Fasten off.

BAG FRONT AND BACK

Arrange the motifs to create 2 equal-sized walls for the back and front of the bag. For the bag pictured, there are 3 motifs across and 4 down. The arrangement of motifs will depend on the size of your bag. Then, using MC, and matching up stitches of squares, either sew (overstitch) the motifs together with a tapestry needle, or single crochet the motifs together.

Once your motifs are joined, measure each whole crocheted piece against the side of your commercial tote. It is good if the crocheted piece is a tad smaller than the actual tote. With a steam iron, lightly steam the crocheted pieces to fit your commercial tote. Set aside.

STRIPED SIDE PANELS (MAKE 2)

With MC, chain 29 (or to match the depth of the bag). Single crochet in the second chain from the hook and into each chain to end—28 stitches.

ROWS 1-4: Chain 2, single crochet in 28 stitches. Fasten off.

ROWS 5-8: Using a new color, repeat Rows 1-4. Continue in this manner, varying yarn colors to your liking, until you have approximately 19 stripes, 18" (46cm) or just under the length of the side of your commercial tote bag, ending with a MC stripe. Fasten off.

BASE OF TOTE

Join any color yarn to one end of a striped side panel. Single crochet 28 stitches across. Work in single crochet until you have just less than 12" (30.5cm) across, approximately 36 rows (or to match the width of the bag). Fasten off, leaving a long tail.

With the tapestry needle and tail, sew the base to the other side panel.

ASSEMBLING TOTE

Matching up corners, pin the front granny motif panels of the tote to the striped side panels. Using the MC, single crochet together along the front side of the tote, joining sides and bottom panels to front. This will also create a piped edge for the bag. Fasten off. Repeat on the opposite side.

CONTRAST CROCHETED PIPING

NOTE: A contrast color piping, while not required, creates a more finished look. Using a contrast color yarn, and starting anywhere at the bottom of the striped side section, slip your hook through any exposed top loop as close as possible to the joining edging. Single crochet around the entire striped section, including the top and bottom edge. When you reach your starting point, join and fasten off. Repeat for the other side.

ATTACHING CROCHETED PIECE TO COMMERCIAL TOTE

Place the commercial tote inside the crocheted piece and use binder clips to clip the crocheted piece to the commercial tote. (Your crocheted bag is essentially a cover for your commercial tote bag.) Make sure the outer bag corners match up to the inner bag corners and that handles are symmetrically positioned.

TOP EDGE OF BAG

Join MC to top edge at center of striped side panel and single crochet around top edge. Remove and replace binder clips, as you progress through an area. Work a second round of single crochet. To make a space for the handles, chain 6 behind the base of the handle, skip 5 stitches in front of handle, and continue to single crochet to the next handle base. Proceed in the same manner all the way around, creating these chains encircling each handle. When you reach your starting point, join and fasten off. With a sewing needle and matching thread, sew the granny cover to the top edge of the grocery bag, using an overstitch. Fasten off.

PART III

CRAFTING FO

To keep someone warm, to comfort a person in pain, to delight a child—these are only a few of the possible motivations for crafters to knit, crochet, quilt, or sew, and then give away what they've created to someone they've never even met. Nothing epitomizes craft, activism, and the spirit of community better. As Ann Rubin, founder of Afghans for Afghans, observes, when a knitter "sees someone in need, a knitter thinks, 'What can I make you?' It's a natural response."

This is not a new phenomenon. Volunteers have been knitting for soldiers and sailors for more than a century. But the ability to galvanize crafters around the country and beyond has been multiplied immeasurably by the powers of the Internet. Asking a favor of your sewing circle has morphed into posting a notice on your blog and having word ricochet around the globe.

The results can be staggering. And it has moved beyond providing crafted objects to enlisting the financial support of a like-minded but far-flung craft community. Stephanie Pearl-McPhee—who writes the popular Yarn Harlot blog—founded Tricoteuses Sans Frontieres/Knitters Without Borders as a response to the Southeast Asian tsunami of December 26, 2004, and began soliciting donations for Doctors Without Borders. At last count she had raised $1,062,217 from sympathetic crafters.

But many of us still long to fashion something out of wool or fabric and imagine the literal and figurative warmth it will bring a stranger. For that there are international efforts, national campaigns, and local projects—or you can identify a need and organize your fellow crafters to answer it. The pleasure it will bring you will be palpable.

R A CAUSE

KNITTERS UNITED

THE RED SCARF PROJECT

EVERY FEBRUARY, SOME 2,500 COLLEGE students around the United States open one of their three-a-year care packages from the Orphan Foundation of America and pull out a red scarf hand-knitted or crocheted by a stranger. For these kids—all of whom have aged out of the foster care system and are now on scholarship for their postsecondary education—the scarf is a sign that someone, somewhere cares about them. For the rest of us, the Red Scarf Project signals the power of the online knitting and crochet community to do good.

The project dates back to 2004, when OFA, which raises awareness of and advocates nationally for thousands of foster teens, was invited to receive scarves that had been entered in a contest sponsored by the Craft Yarn Council. Annalisa Assaadi, then the national events director of OFA, recognized the possibility and effectiveness of a larger-scale effort.

"Charity knitting was emerging," she remembers. "All the stars were aligned." OFA formed a red scarf committee, and in November she began e-mailing knitting groups and bloggers that donations would be welcome.

Among those who heard about the project was Norma Miller, who writes the NowNormaKnits blog from her home in St. Albans, Vermont. Norma hadn't actually been knitting all that long herself. Her mother had taught her to cast on, knit, and purl when she was in junior high, but she hadn't picked up knitting needles again until 2003, when her own teenage daughter wanted to knit a scarf. Then "I got bitten by the bug," Norma says.

The blogging became part of her life a year later. She had been participating in a coffee shop

> *"Never before has there been a medium more appropriate for rallying a cause."*

writing group, trying to work on a short story and running into writer's block. She thought the blog "might open the writing floodgates."

As it turned out, the blog had no effect on the progress of the short story. But it did generate a new network of friends. "I found people who were my peers intellectually and with the same interests," she says, "and then it mushroomed."

When she heard that the Orphan Foundation was asking for contributions of handmade

Norma knits—and blogs—from her living room in Vermont. Thanks to the Internet, she can connect with knitters thousands of miles away for a charitable cause.

scarves, Norma passed the message along, returning to the subject again and again in her posts. It wasn't long before an initial trickle of scarves turned into a deluge at OFA's northern Virginia headquarters.

At first the donations included used scarves, scarves made out of old pot holders stitched together, even scarves made of pillowcases. OFA, however, was looking for things that would make the students feel important. "Foster youth always get secondhand things—hand-me-downs," Annalisa says. With the Red Scarf Project, "We wanted to give them art."

"We're not going for quantity but for quality," notes Lynn Davis, OFA's manager for community partnerships. "We want a scarf that someone will be amazed by."

Adds Norma, "Someone said we need more scarves with 'oooh' and less 'uhhhh.'"

They set up guidelines: Scarves could be knitted or crocheted. They had to be long enough to tie, unisex in style, and red—though that could mean fire-engine, berry, crimson, maroon, or any other shade of red.

They finally succeeded in getting the message across. Lynn estimates that 35,000 scarves have been given out since 2005. Norma, meanwhile, continues her efforts, despite the demands of a regular job. Working out of a modest office in the farmhouse-style home she

Think Local

Charity begins at home, it's said. If you and your knitting group, crocheting friends, or quilt guild want to concentrate on your own community and promote your own cause, you can take tips from those who've organized similar campaigns.

DECIDE HOW MANY PEOPLE YOU ARE TRYING—AND ARE ABLE—TO SERVE. In St. Paul, Minnesota, **Theresa Gaffey**, who works at The Yarnery, notes that the shop began its fall mitten project because the public schools had a large immigrant population who weren't used to the state's harsh winter climate. The shop "ends up being a magnet for people asking for help," she says.

USE ONLINE AS WELL AS IN-PERSON CONTACTS TO PROMOTE YOUR EFFORTS. "We put a notice in our e-newsletter, on the shop Web site, and on our blog," Theresa adds.

CALL SCHOOLS OR CHURCHES TO IDENTIFY GROUPS THAT HAVE THE ABILITY TO DISTRIBUTE ITEMS. "I knew there was a need," says **Jean Lee** of Portland, Maine, who organized Nest to provide hand-knitted hats and mittens to a northern Maine town that experienced severe flooding. "You should just keep calling—respectfully—even if they don't return your phone calls, until you find someone who is overjoyed to hear from you."

REALIZE THAT, FOR SOME PEOPLE, CHARITY KNITTING IS A WAY TO CONNECT. Talking to contributors is important, says Theresa. "It's fun for both sides."

DON'T SEND WHAT'S NOT NEEDED, BUT DO FIND OUT WHAT IS. "Knitters and crocheters are always very quick to fill a need once they know it's there," says **Claire Wudowsky**, a founder of Knitters & Crocheters Care, which acts as a clearinghouse for yarn and knitted items in the Washington, D.C., area. "People never cease to amaze me."

shares with her husband, David, and her ever-present Yorkshire terrier, Mr. Jefferies, she keeps up her daily blog as well as a second Red Scarf site. She knits from the stash of yarn that's "scattered all over the darn place," and she also fits in trips to the OFA office, where she's met other volunteers as well as recipients of the scarves. Chronicling those experiences on her blog keeps the message fresh.

By September every year she's in high gear, helped by friends like designer Anne Hanson, who has set up an ongoing knit-along. "We accept scarves from September 1 to December 15. And I run a fund-raiser, so I'll start collecting prizes for donors—yarn, patterns, books about knitting. The cash goes directly to OFA. It's intended to be a discretionary fund for students' emergencies. These kids have no parents to call."

The popularity of knitting blogs and the strength of the online knitting and crocheting community have continued to propel the project. "Never before has there been a medium more appropriate for rallying a cause," she notes.

As for the result, every Valentine's Day several thousand college students struggling to make it on their own can tie a precious scarf around their neck.

If you knit, crochet, sew, quilt, or all of the above, you can undoubtedly find a group that fits your passions and that would be delighted to have your help. Here are a few ideas to start you thinking . . . and crafting.

For almost a decade, **AFGHANS FOR AFGHANS**, a humanitarian and educational people-to-people project in the San Francisco Bay Area, has worked with experienced relief agencies, transporting thousands of hand-knit and crocheted blankets, sweaters, vests, hats, mittens, and socks to the people of Afghanistan as a gesture of respect and friendship. Founder Ann Rubin explains how and why the group got its start in 2001: "We have the largest Afghan-American community in the country, and the American Friends Service Committee was shipping the first container of blankets to Peshawar before the fall of the Taliban." In addition, they had local dot-com talent to build a Web site to get the word out. The organization has stayed decidedly nonpolitical, while sending beautiful and practical gifts lovingly made by volunteers. "We do what we do because we're determined to remember the Afghan people as long as the need exists," Ann says. The group's timed campaigns target specific items. "It's important to give what's needed," she emphasizes, "not what you want to give."

Unemployment, poverty, health, and social issues—to say nothing of extreme weather—are some of the difficulties facing many of the 40,000 members of the Oglala Sioux Tribe on the Pine Ridge Reservation in South Dakota. Working with an array of social service organizations to provide assistance is **FRIENDS OF THE PINE RIDGE RESERVATION**, which welcomes individual and group contributions of knit, crocheted, and sewn items. The list of what's needed ranges from baby clothes to bed capes for elders, from sweaters to accessories.

A family of volunteers sorts scarves sent by far-flung crafters to the Red Scarf Project.

It is a textile monument of overwhelming proportions: The **AIDS QUILT** is composed of almost 5,800 blocks 12 feet (3.6m) square, with eight 3-by-6-foot (91cm x 183cm) panels making up each block. Every square memorializes a person lost to the disease.

The project dates back to 1985, when gay rights activist Cleve Jones posted placards with the names of AIDS victims on a wall. Thinking it resembled a patchwork quilt, Jones created a panel and with others went on to form the NAMES Project Foundation in 1987 to raise funds and boost awareness. As groups around the country responded with additional panels, the quilt grew. Initially 1,920 panels were displayed on the National Mall in Washington, D.C., but that was just the beginning. Today the quilt is made of panels from every state and twenty-eight nations; the foundation has raised more than $3 million for AIDS-related organizations, and more than 14 million people have come to see the quilt and hear a reading of the names of those it remembers.

The massive work was last shown in its entirety in 1996, but groups of blocks continue to go on display in museums, colleges, and community centers.

Granddaddy (or should we say grandma) of all the volunteer knitting/crocheting programs is **CHRISTMAS AT SEA**, which has been sending seafarers handmade hats, scarves, socks, and other gifts since 1898. Run by the Seamen's Church Institute in New York City, an advocacy group, Christmas at Sea distributes some 17,000 gift packages a year to mariners on the oceans and on inland waterways.

Children with HIV/AIDS in emerging nations are the focus of the **MOTHER BEAR PROJECT**, which has sent 48,650 hand-knit bears around the world to date. The animals are all made from the same pattern but are dressed individually and tagged by each maker as a sign of love for youngsters around the world who have little else.

The **QUILTS OF VALOR FOUNDATION** states its mission as covering all war wounded and injured service members and veterans, whether suffering from physical or psychological wounds. Quilters can contribute finished quilts or send in pieced tops and backing to be finished by "longarmers."

ON THE QUAD SCARF

DESIGNED BY Rebecca Hatcher   **SKILL LEVEL** Easy

When Rebecca Hatcher designed On the Quad, she knew she had to match all the requirements for the OFA's Red Scarf project: a scarf that looks good on both genders, suits a success-bound college student, is between 5" and 8" (12.5–20.5cm) wide, approximately 60" (152.5cm) long, *and* can fold up to fit into a flat mailing box. She created a reversible, worsted-weight pattern with a dynamic grid of rectangles and lines. The unusual three slipped stitches on the edges resemble i-cord piping.

SIZE

One size, 8 ½" x 60" (21.5cm x 152.5cm)

MATERIALS

2 skeins Berroco Ultra Alpaca yarn, 50% Super Fine Alpaca, 50% Peruvian Wool, 3½ oz (400g), 215 yd (197m) in Chianti

TOOLS

Size U.S. 8 (5mm) needles, or size to obtain gauge

GAUGE

16 stitches and 28 rows = 4" (10cm) in box pattern, after blocking. Gauge is not crucial.

STITCH GUIDE

Slip 3 wyif (slip 3 stitches with yarn in front): [Insert the right needle into the stitch purlwise and transfer the stitch from the left needle to the right needle without working it] 3 times. Bring the yarn in front of the 3 stitches and proceed with the next stitch.

BOX PATTERN

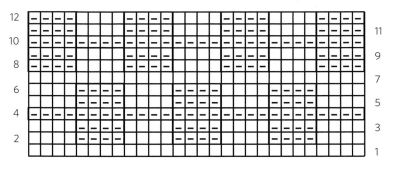

KNIT ON RS, PURL ON WS

PURL ON RS, KNIT ON WS

NOTE: All rows should be started with slip 3 wyif, then proceed to work the chart. After finishing the chart for each row, k3. This applies to both RS and WS. These stitches form a narrow, lengthwise border on either side of the box pattern.

BOX PATTERN

ROW 1 (RS):Knit

ROW 2 (WS): *P4, k4; repeat from* twice, p4.

ROW 3: *K4, p4; repeat from* twice, k4.

ROW 4: Knit.

ROW 5: *K4, p4; repeat from* twice, k4.

ROW 6: *P4, k4; repeat from* twice, p4.

ROW 7: Knit.

ROW 8: *K4, p4; repeat from* twice, k4.

ROW 9: *P4, k4; repeat from* twice, p4.

ROW 10: Knit.

ROW 11: *P4, K4; repeat from* twice, p4.

ROW 12: *K4, p4; repeat from* twice, k4.

Repeat rows 1-12 for pattern

SCARF

Cast on 34 stitches.

RIB BORDER

ROW 1 (WS): Slip 3 wyif *k4, p4; repeat from* twice, k7.

ROW 2 (RS): Slip 3 wyif, *p4, k4; repeat from* twice, p4, k3.

Repeat these 2 rows until the work measures 3" (7.5cm) from the cast-on end, ending with a WS row.

SET-UP ROW (RS): Slip 3 wyif, work in box pattern to the last 3 stitches, k3.

Work in box pattern, slipping 3 stitches at the beginning of each row as established, until scarf measures 57" (145cm) or 3" (7.5cm) less than desired length, ending after row 1.

Work 2 rows of rib border for 3" (7.5cm).

FINISHING

Bind off all stitches and weave in ends. Gently block scarf until squared.

FUSSY CUTS BLANKET

DESIGNED BY Ann Shayne and Kay Gardiner of Mason-Dixon Knitting   **SKILL LEVEL** Intermediate

Ann Shayne and Kay Gardiner have been vocal champions of Afghans for Afghans, so we asked them to design a group afghan project in their inimitable Mason-Dixon style. They chose to show off the quirky color changes in Noro Silk Garden yarn and cleverly managed to avoid the often tedious seaming of putting it all together. At one skein per square, it's ideal for knitters who want to contribute to a project that can be donated to a cause. Of course, the finished blanket is also luxurious enough to be a fine fund-raising item.

The blanket is composed of 20 log cabin blocks. While the blocks are uniform in their finished size and similar in construction, they are not identical. Each block will be different, mainly because Noro Silk Garden is a self-striping yarn with many gradations of color and no clear rhythm to the color repeats, but also because the proportions of the squares vary. The pattern specifies 3 block styles. Each style starts with a different-size center square, knit in one of the brighter or more contrasting colors found in each skein of Silk Garden.

The sample blanket uses 9 style 1 blocks, 4 style 2 blocks, and 7 style 3 blocks. Once you've knit a block or two, you will understand how you can vary the proportions and still end up with the same finished block size, and you can free yourself from the pattern instructions. Making up a design as you go along is one of the joys of log cabin knitting.

Because knitters can never leave "stunning enough" alone, Ann and Kay expect (and hope) to see versions of this blanket in many other yarns. A version using solid or semicolors, instead of a self-striping yarn, would have graphic pop.

What they don't advise is to send a large group of knitters into their stashes to cull yarn for these blocks, unless you're looking for a scrappy mishmash of a blanket. (Not that there's anything wrong with a scrappy mishmash! Ann and Kay love a scrappy mishmash! But that's not the idea here.) Set some rules about the yarn specifications and gauge, unleash your knitters, and you'll get a museum-worthy textile every time.

FINISHED MEASUREMENTS

20-square afghan: 52" x 64¾" (133cm x 164cm)

Square: approximately 12¾" x 12¾" (32.5cm x 32.5cm)

MATERIALS

20 skeins Noro Silk Garden, 45% Silk, 45% Kid Mohair, 10% Lambswool, 1¾ oz (50g), 109 yd (100m) in assorted colors (You could also do this in repeating or single colorways.)

10 skeins Brown Sheep Lamb's Pride Worsted, 85% Wool, 15% Mohair, 4 oz (113g), 190 yd (173m) in Café au Lait

NOTE ABOUT YARN QUANTITIES: It is easy to adjust the size of the blanket by knitting more or fewer squares. Each square uses almost 1 skein of Noro Silk Garden, and the framing takes a little less than half a skein of the Brown Sheep Lamb's Pride Worsted. So a 16-square blanket would require 16 skeins of Silk Garden and 8 skeins of Brown Sheep Lamb's Pride Worsted; a crib-sized blanket composed of 6 squares would take 6 skeins of Noro Silk Garden and 3 skeins of Brown Sheep Lamb's Pride Worsted. Save your leftovers to work the i-cord edging. If you want to be doubly sure that you don't run short, get an extra skein of the Brown Sheep Lamb's Pride.

TOOLS

Size U.S. 6 (4mm) straight needles

Size U.S. 6 (4mm) circular needles with cable length of 24" (61cm) or greater, for joining strips of blocks (You will need at least 2 of these.)

Smooth scrap yarn to hold stitches, or stitch holders, or many spare circular needles

Size U.S. 6 (4mm) double-pointed needles—set of 5 (optional)

Tapestry needle

Stitch markers (4 in all; one of which is distinguishable from the other 3)

GAUGE

20 stitches and 40 rows (20 garter ridges) = 4" (10cm) in garter stitch

NOTE: The specific gauge is not critical; the important thing is for the gauge of the blocks to be consistent from one to the next. Also, be sure to check your gauge on *both* yarns and change needles as necessary.

STITCH GUIDE

I-CORD: Using 2 double-pointed needles, cast on the required number of stitches (usually 3 or 4). *Without turning the work, slide the stitches to the right end of the needle, pull the yarn across the back of the work and knit the stitches. Repeat from * until the cord is the desired length.

BLANKET

Following the instructions below, or your own design, and using Noro Silk Garden, make 20 log cabin blocks in varying styles, but all the same size.

LOG CABIN BLOCK, STYLE 1

This is the basic block. It starts with a center square that is 16 stitches wide by 16 garter ridges long. The reason the center patch is square is because of the immortal truth of garter stitch: 1 stitch = 1 garter ridge (which is composed of 2 rows of garter stitch).

The center patch is then surrounded with 4 log cabin strips, each of which is 16 garter ridges long. The resulting block (before framing, as specified later in the instructions) will be 48 combined stitches and garter ridges wide, by 48 combined stitches and garter ridges long.

To begin, look at your skein of Silk Garden. Typically, there will be several shades of one or two main colors, interspersed with shorter lengths of a bright or contrasting color (the "contrast color"); some colorways have these short bursts of more than one contrast color. To make the blocks in the sample blanket, Ann and Kay started by finding one of the contrast colors in the skein and physically cutting it out. (When quilters do this with fabric, they call it "fussy cutting.") Knitting the center patch in a contrast color on all (or most) of the center squares will give the blanket more visual interest and rhythm. (If you don't like the effect of the centers "popping," don't fussy-cut. Just start knitting with the beginning of the skein like a normal person.)

Center Patch

Using the contrast color of your choice and size

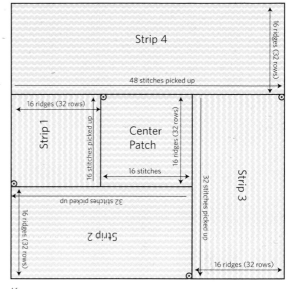

Key

⊙ = Last live stitch in section

6 (4mm) needles, cast on 16 stitches. Work 16 garter ridges by knitting 32 rows (knit every row), and bind off on the right side, leaving the last stitch live.

Strip 1

Break off the contrast color. For the rest of the block, use the main skein and do not cut the yarn until the block is finished.

Turn the work 1 quarter-turn to the right, with the right side facing, and pick up and knit 1 stitch in each of the 16 garter ridges—17 stitches.
NEXT ROW (WS): Knit to the last 2 stitches (one of which is the stitch that was left live after binding off the center patch), k2tog—16 stitches.
Knit 15 more garter ridges, and bind off on the right side, leaving the last stitch live.

Strip 2

Turn the work 1 quarter-turn to the right, with the right side facing, and pick up and knit 1 stitch in each of the 16 garter ridges of Strip 1 and in each of the stitches on the cast-on edge of the center patch. (This may require some fudging and futzing, but be sure you pick up 16 stitches on the cast-on edge—33 stitches.)

NEXT ROW (WS): Knit to the last 2 stitches (one of which is the stitch that was left live after binding off Strip 1), k2tog—32 stitches.

Knit 15 more garter ridges, and bind off on the right side, leaving the last stitch live.

Strip 3

Turn the work 1 quarter-turn to the right, with the right side facing, and pick up and knit 1 stitch in each of the 16 garter ridges of Strip 2 and in each of the 16 garter ridges of the center patch—33 stitches.

NEXT ROW (WS): Knit to the last 2 stitches (one of which is the stitch that was left live after binding off Strip 2), k2tog—32 stitches.

Knit 15 more garter ridges, and bind off on the right side, leaving the last stitch live.

Strip 4

Turn the work 1 quarter-turn to the right, with the right side facing, and pick up and knit 1 stitch in each of the 16 garter ridges of Strip 3, in each of the 16 stitches of the cast-off edge of the center patch, and in each of the 16 garter ridges of Strip 1—49 stitches.

NEXT ROW (WS): Knit to the last 2 stitches (one of which is the stitch that was left live after binding off Strip 3), k2tog—48 stitches.

Knit 15 more garter ridges, and bind off all stitches on the right side. Weave in the ends.

Instructions for block styles 2 and 3 assume that you are familiar with how block style 1 is constructed and will not repeat all the instructions. All the blocks are worked in the same manner, specifically:

1. Center patch is knitted in a contrast color.

2. Center patch is surrounded with 4 strips using the main skein of yarn.

3. When the center patch and strips 1, 2, and 3 are bound off, 1 stitch is left live.

4. On the second row (WS) of strips 1, 2, 3, and 4, the last 2 stitches are knitted together to maintain the correct stitch count.

What differs is the size of the center patch and the number of rows for each of the surrounding strips. You can mess with this as much as you like, as long as you end up with a block that is 48 stitches and ridges by 48 stitches and ridges and measures approximately 9 ¾" x 9 ¾" (25cm x 25cm).

LOG CABIN BLOCK, STYLE 2

CENTER PATCH: Cast on 12 stitches, knit 16 garter ridges.

STRIP 1: Pick up 16 stitches, knit 18 garter ridges.

STRIP 2: Pick up 30 stitches, knit 16 garter ridges.

STRIP 3: Pick up 32 stitches, knit 18 garter ridges.

STRIP 4: Pick up 48 stitches, knit 16 garter ridges.

LOG CABIN BLOCK, STYLE 3

CENTER PATCH: Cast on 6 stitches, knit 6 garter ridges, do not bind off. Change to another contrast color and knit 18 garter ridges—total of 24 garter ridges.

STRIP 1: Pick up 24 stitches, knit 21 garter ridges.

STRIP 2: Pick up 27 stitches, knit 12 garter ridges.

LOG CABIN BLOCK, STYLE 2

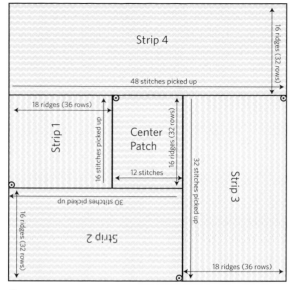

Key

⊙ = Last live stitch in section

LOG CABIN BLOCK, STYLE 3

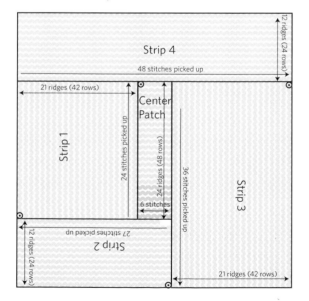

Key

⊙ = Last live stitch in section
〰 = Color 1
〰 = Color 2

STRIP 3: Pick up 36 stitches, knit 21 ridges.

STRIP 4: Pick up 48 stitches, knit 12 ridges.

FRAMING THE BLOCKS

Each of the 20 blocks will now be framed with a mitered border, knit in the round. The borders are not bound off, leaving live stitches. The framed blocks are then joined into strips by working a 3-needle bind-off on adjoining edges. The strips are then joined by the same method, binding off the live stitches along each edge of joined blocks. This will leave the blanket with 4 long edges of live stitches. The blanket is finished by working an i-cord bind off around this entire edge. Seamless. Perfect. Pretty dang cool.

With the right side of the log cabin block facing, and using either 2 size 6 (4mm) circular needles, a single circular, or a set of 5 double-pointed needles (this is a matter of personal preference) and the solid color yarn, pick up 48 stitches on each edge of the block, placing a marker at each corner, and the distinctive marker at the end, to mark the beginning of the round.

Working garter stitch in the round (knit 1 round, purl 1 round), work 7 garter ridges, increasing 2 stitches at each corner on every "knit" round, as follows:

ROUND 1: Knit into the front and back (kfb) of the first stitch,*knit to 1 stitch before the marker, kfb, slip marker, kfb; repeat from * until round is complete.

ROUND 2: Purl.

Repeat these 2 rounds 6 more times, for a total of 7 garter ridges. Because you are increasing 2 stitches on each side every time you work Round 1, you will end up with 62 stitches on each edge of the frame, and a total of 248 stitches. Break the yarn. Leave the stitches on each side of the frame on separate lengths of scrap yarn, holders, or spare double-pointed needles.

ASSEMBLY

The squares can be framed and joined one at a time, or you can frame them all before deciding on your layout and the order of joining them. Play with the layout; throw your framed squares on the ground randomly and then tweak it a little. Rotate a square a quarter-turn. But don't get too fussy: These squares will look good together no matter what you do. Joining is a good task for a well-organized group, or the most intense knitter in the group; you decide.

After choosing your layout scheme, assemble the framed blocks into 4 strips of 5 blocks each, using a 3-needle bind-off, as follows:

Set up the 2 edges to be joined by placing the 62 stitches of each edge onto 2 circular needles. Line up 2 blocks with right sides facing each other, and using a third needle and the frame color, work a 3-needle bind-off as follows: Insert working needle into the front of the first stitch on each of the 2 edges, knit the 2 stitches together, *insert the working needle into the front of the next stitch on each of the 2 edges, knit the 2 stitches together, pass the first stitch over the second stitch; repeat from * until all the stitches are bound off. Break yarn and fasten off the last stitch.

Once you have assembled the strips, join the strips to each other by working a 3-needle bind-off using the 2 circular needles with longer cables. (Each strip of 5 blocks will have 310 stitches.)

Weave in all ends, closing any small holes at the corners as you do this.

I-CORD EDGING

The edging on the sample blanket is worked almost entirely in the solid color, with a couple of short bursts of contrasting colors from the left-over Noro Silk Garden (because it's fun to do this).

Starting on any edge of the blanket, position a circular needle in the live stitches, so that they are ready to be bound off. On a separate (short) needle, cast on 3 stitches (use a provisional cast-on if you want to be fancy and graft the i-cord together at the end), and transfer them to the circular needle holding the edge stitches. Work as follows: *k2, k2tog through the back loops (thus joining the i-cord stitches together with 1 edge stitch), place the 3 stitches on the right-hand needle back onto the left-hand needle; repeat from * to end of stitches. This is a long, meditative, and deeply satisfying journey.

NOTE: At each corner, work 2 rounds of i-cord without joining it to an edge stitch; this will ease the i-cord around the corners, helping them to lie flat.

When you get back to where you started the i-cord, bind off, and join the beginning and end of the i-cord with a few deft stitches using your tapestry needle. If you opted for a provisional cast-on, undo it and graft the i-cord ends together however you like to graft things together, ya big, perfectionist nut. (Ann and Kay say that with love.) All that is needed now is a final inspection to ensure that you have left no ends dangling, and a light steam with the steam iron. Savor the moment. Tweet it to the world.

SLEIGHT OF HANDS MITTENS

DESIGNED BY Mary Lou Egan   **SKILL LEVEL** Intermediate

Mary Lou Egan was involved with a mitten project at her local St. Paul, Minnesota, yarn store. Her creations offer a real smorgasbord of possibilities. Choose one of the six patterns—or a solid color rib—for the cuff and then combine it with any other pattern for the hand portion. While they look complicated, these are actually simple repeats that require only two shades of yarn to be worked on any row, so they are a great introduction to stranded color knitting.

SIZE
Child Small (Child Medium/Adult Small, Adult Medium)

FINISHED MEASUREMENTS
Palm circumference: 6 ¼ (7 ½, 8 ½)" (16 [19, 21.5] cm)
Length: Approximately 7 ¼ (8 ¾, 10)" (18.5 [22, 25.5]cm)

TOOLS
1 skein Louet Gems Sport Weight, 100% Merino Wool, 3½ oz (100g), 225 yd (205m) in each color required (approximately 115 [150, 270] total yards per pair [105 (137, 247)]).

NOTE: The actual amount of specific colors will vary, due the variety of ways to make the mittens.

TOOLS
Size U.S. 4 (3.5mm) double-pointed or long circular needles, or size to get gauge

GAUGE
26 stitches and 30 rows = 4" (10cm) in 2-color stockinette st.
Charts are interchangeable for each size, either cuff or hand. Begin at the lower right of chosen pattern and work the number of repeats required for the particular size.

CUFF

Choose between a single-color rib, or any of the colorwork charts.

With MC, cast on 40 (48, 56) stitches.

Place marker and join, being careful not to twist the cast-on.

Divide the stitches evenly for the front and the back. If using double-pointed needles, place 20 (24, 28) stitches onto one needle, place marker, and place 10 (12, 14) stitches on each of the two needles. If using 1 long circular needle, place 20 (24, 28) stitches on front, place marker, and place 20 (24, 28) stitches on back.

RIBBED CUFF

*K1, p1, repeat from * to end. Continue for 20 rounds total or approximately 2" (5cm).

COLORWORK CUFF

Purl 3 rounds. With MC, knit 1 round.
FLOWER CHART: work 15 rounds
2-COLOR TRIANGLE CHART AND 3-COLOR
GRID CHART: work 18 rounds
DIAGONALS CHART: work 12 rounds
ZIG-ZAG CHART: work 19 rounds
TRIANGLES CHART: work 16 rounds
With MC, knit one round.
Choose chart for hand.

HAND

Work to 24 (30, 34) rounds of chosen chart, or until piece measures approximately 3¼ (3¾, 4½)" (8 [9.5, 11.5]cm) from the cast-on edge.

THUMB SETUP
Right-Hand Mitten

With scrap yarn, k8 (10, 12), slip these stitches back onto the left needle, continue in established pattern to end.

Left-Hand Mitten

Work 12 (14, 16) stitches in chart pattern, with scrap yarn, k8 (10, 12), slip these stitches, back onto the left needle, and continue in established pattern to end.

Work another 22 (26, 30) rounds in established pattern, or until piece measures approximately 6½ (7½, 8½)" (16.5 [19, 21.5]cm) from the cast-on edge, or to desired length.

DECREASE FOR TIP

NOTE: Work the decrease stitches in the MC of the row. Work the center stitch between decreases in the contrast color.

Decrease round, *Ssk, work in pattern to 3 stitches before the marker, k2tog, k1, slip marker; repeat from * once.

Repeat the decrease round every round until 8 stitches remain. Break off yarns, draw the end through the stitches, and fasten off.

THUMB

Remove the scrap yarn while placing the 8 (10, 12) front of the thumb stitches onto 1 double-pointed needle, and the 7 (9, 11) back of thumb stitches onto another needle. Pick up 1 extra stitch at the end of the back set of stitches—16 (20, 24) stitches. Pick up and twist a loop at each side of the thumb opening—18 (22, 26) stitches. Work the front of the thumb following the chart for the hand and work the back of the thumb in 1-stitch stripes, alternating between MC and the contrasting color of that round.

Work 12 (16, 18) rounds total, or to desired length. With MC, begin decreasing for tip of thumb as follows:
ROUND 1: [K2tog, k1] 4 (5, 6) times, k0 (1, 0)—8 (11, 12) stitches.
ROUND 2: Knit.

ROUND 3: [K2tog] 4 (5, 6) times, k0 (1, 0)—4 (6, 6) stitches.
Break off yarn, draw through stitches on needle and fasten off. Tidy up sides of thumb.
Weave in ends.

FLOWER CHART

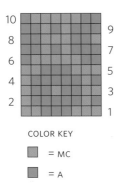

10
8
6
4
2

9
7
5
3
1

COLOR KEY

■ = MC

■ = A

2-COLOR TRIANGLE CHART

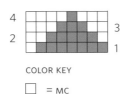

4
2

3
1

COLOR KEY

□ = MC

■ = A

3-COLOR TRIANGLES CHART

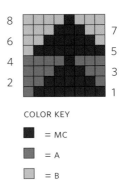

8
6
4
2

7
5
3
1

COLOR KEY

■ = MC

■ = A

■ = B

GRID CHART

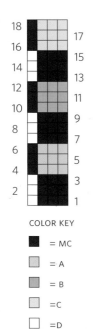

18
16
14
12
10
8
6
4
2

17
15
13
11
9
7
5
3
1

COLOR KEY

■ = MC

■ = A

■ = B

■ =C

□ =D

DIAGONALS CHART

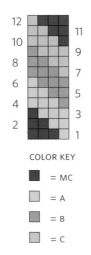

12
10
8
6
4
2

11
9
7
5
3
1

COLOR KEY

■ = MC

□ = A

■ = B

□ = C

ZIG-ZAG CHART

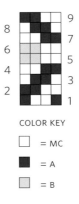

8
6
4
2

9
7
5
3
1

COLOR KEY

□ = MC

■ = A

■ = B

PART IV

CRAFTING TO RENEW AND REUSE

The entire DIY movement begins with a "green" impulse: Making something yourself, after all, as opposed to buying it ready-made, is your first step toward sustainability, and artists and crafters have been repurposing since long before the concept became trendy. There's a notable tradition of found objects in art, and thrifty women have always been adept at reusing materials already at hand. Rag rugs and patchwork quilts were our grandmothers' versions of recycling.

Today, among other things, we've got *trashion*, a catchy name for an urban trend of making—and promoting—runway-worthy clothes and jewelry out of someone else's discards. Other savvy designers simply call what they do *upcycling*—using pieces from their wardrobes and refashioning them into hip, new clothes, accessories, or home décor. Buying vintage from local secondhand stores—which just might harbor a trove of all wool sweaters or 100 percent cotton dresses—makes an affordable and easy statement about trimming one's carbon footprint to the size of the neighborhood. And now forward-looking designers have even begun to talk about *slow design*—the belief that how a garment is made is as important as what it's made of—along with sustainability.

RECYCLE,

As crafters have demanded—and manufacturers have responded with—eco-friendly products, debate has sprung up on what that term means, what the results are, and what guidelines craft consumers can use. Questions abound: For example, do you support local businesses (a hallmark of sustainability), even if they don't carry all-natural wares? Or do you order "green" products online and have them shipped across the country or even across oceans? Do you prefer natural and organic goods, or are you interested in recycling materials to save space in our landfills?

Recycling also touches on the health of the environment. Troubled by the proliferation of plastic bags in the world? You can use them to make something else: plastic fabric, a permanent tote bag, or, better yet, art or craft that is itself a comment on our tendency toward overconsumption. There's no denying that packaging has become a sophisticated marketer's tool, with colors, typefaces, and messages cleverly designed to persuade the buyer to buy more. Reworking those bags, cans, and bottle caps in smile-inducing combinations is creative reuse at its best.

RECYCLED CHIC

CRISPINA ffRENCH

CRISPINA ffRENCH JOKES THAT SHE WANTS to change the world. Or perhaps she's not joking. Take the name of the town she lives in, Pittsfield, in western Massachusetts. Crispina is determined to retitle the place Shire City. "*Pittsfield* has negative connotations," she says, a stigma from its old industrial associations. "*Shire City* sounds pretty. I try to impart a positive spin on it."

Creating something beautiful out of unlikely materials is what she excels in. For nearly two decades, she had a business based on recycled wool sweaters. For her more recent design workshops, she produces eye-catching clothes, blankets, rugs, and soft toylike sculptures from recycled garments. And with her husband and several others, she has "recycled" a former Catholic church and rectory into a home and workshop.

Crispina grew up in Great Barrington, where both her parents taught high school art. "Mom was a fine arts painter," she says. Her father, a highly recognized Irish-born potter and teacher—the lower-case double letter in her last name is a legacy

of his heritage—was the one who "gave me the original idea of using recycled sweaters. I was making felt, a wet cold process, and he said, 'You know, you could just wash sweaters and get the same effect.'"

That was around 1987, when she was finishing an art degree, having recently returned from an apprenticeship with a weaver in British Columbia. Following her father's suggestion, she went to thrift stores, bought sweaters, and used them to make cuddly toys she dubbed Ragamuffins. She also wove cloth, and when she entered her creations in an American Craft Council Fair, she took so many wholesale orders that her design business was born. "I had no

Creating something beautiful out of unlikely materials is what she excels in.

managerial experience," she recalls, but "within two years I had forty employees."

Gradually, she wove less and focused more on recycled fabric, buying thousand-pound (454kg) bales of used sweaters, "though people didn't know what recycling was then." Customers were intrigued by her soft sculptures. "One woman told me, 'Your Ragamuffin looks just like my husband.' (And it did!)" Crispina

Adorable dolls to warm the heart are made from sweaters and other garments that once warmed the body. Crispina sells her popular toys at craft fairs.

also developed blankets and rugs that were woven from waste materials on looms of her own design. When the business closed in 2008, however, she decided to give up on wholesale production.

"Dad asked, 'What are you going to make in the studio?' I said, 'Phone calls and e-mails.' I realized then that I hadn't had an artful experience in a long time. Now I have the ability to be creative."

There were other changes in her life, too. She married Chris Swindlehurst in 2004, and they have two young daughters, Lucy and Violet, along with Crispina's teenage son, Ben. Even before the wedding, Chris—who owns a heating

business and specializes in alternative energies, biodiesel, and photovoltaic cells—encouraged his wife to give up her crumbling, leaky studio in Housatonic, Massachusetts, and find a new place to work.

No one would have expected the place they found, however. A chance encounter at a dinner party led them to Pittsfield's 1895 Notre Dame Church and rectory, which was on the market. "We fell in love with the building," Crispina says. Together with several others, they've turned it into an "intentional living laboratory" that they call the Alchemy Initiative, sponsoring workshops in reconstruction arts and gardening; cultivating an urban farm with raised beds,

Digging for Vintage Treasures

Bridgett Artise has been turning vintage garments into new ones for almost a decade. An author, instructor, and the principal of B. Artise Originals, she still shops at thrift stores like those sponsored by Goodwill and the Salvation Army to find the raw materials for her designs. For those who would follow in her sewing footsteps, she has several tips.

1. When planning a thrift-shop foray, give yourself a whole day. "You have to take time. Don't rush."

2. Pay attention to the labels. The typeface and colors will let you know what's really vintage.

3. Look for interesting textures, patterns, and high-quality, even luxurious fabrics, which are used more rarely now.

4. Watch for vintage design classics. Peter Pan collars can be removed and put on other bodices. Double-knit quilted housecoats can be turned into fabulous jackets. Pleated plaid skirts and wrap skirts can also be reused to great effect.

5. Realize that sizes have changed. A vintage size 10 might fit someone used to wearing size 6 today.

6. Don't be afraid to experiment with outrageous patterns. "I found a double-knit housecoat with an orange and purple mosaiclike design," Bridgett says. "It was hideous as a one-piece, but I turned it into two dresses that are my favorites to this day."

beehives, and chickens; and housing artisan studios in the church basement. "There's no spiritual aspect," she says, "but a set of values. We operate as a group and live in a way that's sustainable and fun."

She's once again busy with her own craft, notably new garments from old cotton T-shirts and dresses. Half the world's people "live where wool is too hot," she acknowledges. "This brings more people into the mind-set of using recycled materials." And for students in her workshops, these are materials that can be picked up inexpensively at Goodwill. "People need things that are cheap that they can make mistakes on."

In 2009, Crispina published *The Sweater Chop Shop*, which she sees as a way of spreading her ideas. "I did a pot-holder rug workshop," she notes, "and the ladies left here on cloud nine because they made a pile of T-shirts into a rug that's simple and beautiful. I'm excited and encouraged by how people have taken to recycling. But there's so much more to do. It still doesn't impact our buying habits. People have so much more power than they realize."

Makers Jam

Knitters who want to work with organic yarns can often find a selection at their local yarn store, and in recent years quilters especially have been requesting eco-friendly fabrics.

NATALIE CHANIN founded Alabama Chanin—which produces limited-edition couture clothes and other lifestyle products—on the principles of sustainability and slow design. The ideas go back to our grandmothers, she notes, "who grew up in a time of no excess. How creative they were with basic materials!" She has tips for home sewers, beginners, and experienced crafters alike:

· Look close to home for materials. "Take a T-shirt and recycle it into your life. I started my company with a recycled T-shirt, when I cut it up and sewed it to make something to wear."

· Don't worry about fancy tools. Start with what you have.

· Be inspired by the example of our grandparents, who "were the greenest people imaginable." They used everything, making pillows from flour sacks and creating redwork embroidery with red thread unraveled from Red Man tobacco pouches.

· Remember that slow design is about *how* you make something and the impact on a community.

Above all, Natalie Chanin says, "Do your due diligence. For example, bamboo is a readily renewable resource, but chemicals that process it aren't good for the environment. And natural dyes sound great, but need heavy metals to fix them, so manmade colors may be better for the environment. Take the time to inform yourself."

NADINE CURTIS, who founded BeSweet, says the key for her was to create "a social business. I found products I was attracted to that were made in an empowering way." BeSweet markets yarns and accessories made by women's groups in South Africa who use indigenous—mostly mohair—fibers, hand-dye and spin the yarns, and then utilize small machines. "I believe in the environment," Nadine adds, "but empowering people who have fewer opportunities is most important."

SUN-TEA DRESSES

DESIGNED BY Crispina ffrench   **SKILL LEVEL** Intermediate

Reuse, Renew, and Recycle are watchwords for Crispina ffrench, who specializes in making appealing outfits out of pieces of old clothing. Here she works her hand-stitched alchemy on T-shirts, turning them into playful sundresses and taking a stand on environmentalism at the same time.

SIZE
To fit

MATERIALS
5 or 6 adult-size cotton T-shirts in a palette that you like
Any commercial pattern designed for knit fabric (Note: The short-sleeve dress shown is Vogue 8489. The strap dress is copied from a garment Crispina owns.)
Embroidery floss in colors that complement the T-shirt colors

TOOLS
Quilters' needles (long and fine)
Sharp fabric scissors
Straight pins

OPTIONAL
Beeswax or Thread Heaven thread conditioner
Leather thimbles for thumb and forefinger
Rotary cutter and self-healing mat

1. SELECTING THE MATERIAL

One of the reasons Crispina uses T-shirts to make other clothing is because they are very common and easy to find. Color selection and "hand"—the drape and feel of the fabric— are generally great and, often, T-shirts hold sentimental value. T-shirts are prevalent in thrift shops. They can be recycled from your dresser, and usually friends are happy to donate some. When choosing your material, consider color, texture, and print placement. If you are trying to include interesting words or logos, you need to cut your pieces carefully.

2. CUTTING

Follow the directions for cutting from the pattern that you have purchased. Do your best to follow pattern grain lines. Do not cut (or worry about) facings or interfacings. Once you get used to it, using a rotary cutter will provide cleaner lines than cutting with scissors. If the garment calls for a zipper, consider cutting the piece on the fold, rather than in 2 separate pieces and adding the zipper later.

3. STITCHING

A simple running stitch is what Crispina uses most often. Separate 2 strands of 6-strand embroidery floss and use it to sew. Treating the floss with beeswax or thread conditioner will reduce friction, help prevent tangling, and allow it to glide through the material more easily. A thimble will make it easier to push the needle through multiple layers of fabric.

For topstitching—sewing that shows to the outside of the garment—you can use a single (or double) row of running stitch, whipstitch, or any other stitch in a matching or contrasting color.

4. SEAMING AND ASSEMBLING

NOTE: The order of assembly is generally the same as the pattern directions, but read through them completely before beginning, just to make sure. Since facings are being eliminated, you'll handle edges differently. Also, since T-shirt knits don't ravel much, you can leave seam allowances and edges unfinished or even raw.

There are two major methods of seaming: In the first method, the seam is sewn with wrong sides together about ⅝" (16mm) from the edge of the cloth. Then, the two raw edges are folded down in the same direction and topstitched in place. This results in the raw edges being on the outside of the garment.

The second method is the reverse: Sew the seams in the same manner, but with *right sides together*. Then fold seams together and topstitch as in the first method. This results in a slightly cleaner look, with the raw edges being on the inside. Usually garments that have a major horizontal seam, such as waistlines and waistbands, are constructed in sections. The top and bottom parts are assembled separately, and then they are joined to each other, or to the waistband, with the second method of seaming, above. To get a clean, smooth look, fold the seam allowances toward the waistband and topstitch.

5. FINISHING

FOR SPAGHETTI STRAPS

Cut a 2" (5cm) strip clear across the body of a T-shirt. Cut it the length you need for the strap. Fold it in half the long way and running-stitch ⅝" (16mm) in from the cut edge. Then fold in half the long way again, matching the two cut edges and the folded edge. Running-stitch again, this time closer to the edges.

TO INSERT ZIPPERS

Place the zipper on the inside of the garment and pin it in place, carefully tucking the top tabs of the zipper under and making the top edge nice and neat. Beginning at the top, stitch 1 side of the zipper in place using a whipstitch or ladder stitch. Secure the bottom of the zipper in place with a decorative X or box stitch and then work your way back to the top with a whipstitch or ladder stitch. Once the zipper is sewn in place, carefully cut down between the two rows of stitches, allowing the zipper to open. If you have to cut across any hand-sewn seams of your dress, be sure that you plan ahead and secure the place that will be cut across with a double stitch and knot on either side so that when you cut the zipper open, you are not running the risk that your dress will fall apart.

FOR EDGES AND HEMS

In place of facings and/or around hems, you can bind with long strips of T-shirt, cut 1" (2.5cm) wide. Fold the 1" (2.5cm) strip around the raw edges and stitch in place using a running stitch. A neatly cut edge can also make a simple, flowing hem.

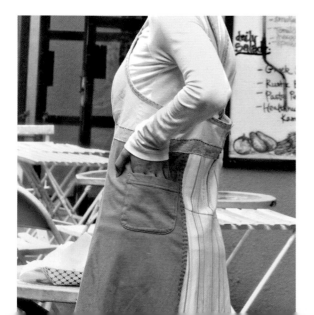

ONE WORD: PLASTIC

VIRGINIA FLECK

MESMERIZING SWIRLS. EYE-OPENING star-bursts. Virginia Fleck's eye-candy mandalas, some of them 9 or 10 feet (2.7m or 3m) in diameter, are meant to overwhelm viewers with their size, color, and design. Only after a sense of "How did she do that?" creeps in does one begin to notice individual elements. Is that a red Target circle? Is that a 7-Eleven smiley face? Can this really be made of recycled plastic bags?

Yes, and yes, and yes. Virginia's creations are not only gorgeous examples of recycling, but they're also her sly comments on consumer culture. She's been intrigued by the artistic reuse of found objects ever since she attended the School of the Museum of Fine Arts in Boston.

"Trash Day in Boston was amazing," remembers Virginia. "People would throw away stuff from the 1950s." Art school trips to government supply warehouses turned up cases of plastic containers and old telephones. "It got me thinking about the social meaning of the objects and gave me an introduction to reuse."

In the early 1990s she and her husband, musician Dan Torosian, moved to the arts-friendly town of Austin, Texas, where her work at first centered on sod-brick sculptures. Then in 2003 an opportunity to exhibit in Cuba—through a local gallery that hosted artist exchanges—pushed her in a new direction.

Spurred by the exhibit theme of "dreams and nightmares," Virginia decided to make a giant pillow. Since carrying art in and out of Cuba posed a problem, she created an inflatable work out of plastic bags. "I scored thousands of bags—all different colors," she says. "I thought I could make it interesting visually." The slogans and promises printed on the plastic both "fascinated and disgusted" her. "There's a lot to those carefully crafted slogans, from colors to type fonts. I hadn't realized how much we were being marketed to."

> *"We need to question what we . . . consume and what we are consumed by."*

She assembled pinwheels and starbursts out of the bags, taped and sewed them together, and packed them in her suitcase. The finished pillow, her version of the American Dream, was inflated by a computer cooler fan and filled the tiny Havana gallery space.

Back home, with plenty of bags left, she tried a second piece. "I did a starburst and tacked it up on the wall. When I came back in and saw it, I thought, 'That's a mandala—a wiseass mandala.'"

CLOCKWISE FROM TOP LEFT: Virginia Fleck's artistry soars in a kitelike flower; in the studio; measuring panels for a circle skirt; smiley-face images contribute to Virginia's serious mandalas.

Since then, Virginia has created many more mandalas, complex circular designs that are tools for meditation used by many traditions. They've certainly made her think, she says, adding, "We all need to question what we want to consume and what we are consumed by."

She begins each work by settling on an overall color palette—warm tones, perhaps, or all black and white—and choosing bags from her collection. With Plexiglas templates and a rotary cutter, "I cut way more than I would ever need," she says, but she never sketches anything in advance. "Things that happen by chance are much more interesting," she says. As she arranges and layers the plastic shapes, she watches to see if a theme develops. "My job is to notice, respond to it, and develop it," she says, highlighting the slogans or logos through graphic design or repeating elements to make a point. The results are held together with layers of ordinary tape, which, she notes, is acid-free and pH-balanced.

You have to see the artworks to gauge the effect. "I make them big on purpose," she says. "Big has an intellectual and physical impact, and I want them to be as manipulative as the ads themselves."

In recent years Virginia has also produced temporary installations like *Laguna Gyre*, a 70-foot (21m) mandala of inflated plastic bags that was sited at a pond's edge and that gradually deflated to evoke the agglomeration of plastic trash whirling in the ocean's North Pacific Gyre.

As a wider consciousness about recycling plastic has grown, Austin's lively art scene has given birth to groups like Austin Creative Reuse and Austin Green Art. Even Virginia's seventeen-year-old daughter, Circe, has banded with friends—self-dubbed the Angsty Teenage

Eco Warriors—and developed plastic-bag craft projects as a way to raise money for Kiva.org, which makes microloans to would-be entrepreneurs around the globe.

Virginia tells the story of a friend's mother who met the Dalai Lama and used the opportunity to ask him about the world's biggest problem and what an artist could do to help. His answer? Make work that shines a light on greed. Virginia insists that she doesn't "want to be didactic or preachy." But she likes to think that she raises some timely questions about consumption. She says, "I want to shine a light on greed."

D.I.Y.

Plabric Anyone?

You probably have a stash in your broom closet or under your sink. Now you can make something useful—or decorative—with those thin plastic bags.

By ironing two or three layers of the plastic between sheets of parchment or wax paper, you can create a new plastic "fabric." (Use a polyester setting and be sure to keep your room well ventilated.) Once you have sheets of plastic to work with, you can sew it like any other cloth.

THE ANGSTY TEENAGE ECO WARRIORS in Austin have come up with a simple design that starts with plastic hardware cloth (a loose netting) from Home Depot. They cut the material into shapes patterned on their favorite bags, wire the pieces together, and then weave strips of colorful plastic bags through the netting.

In New York City, **BAGS FOR THE PEOPLE** began in early 2009 to make simple, reusable, drawstring bags out of old clothes and fabric and to give them out free at weekly green markets. Now the group, headed by Glenn Robinson, concentrates on organizing workshops and events where even beginning sewers can learn to make a bag for themselves and perhaps an extra one to donate. They're at seven thousand bags and counting. The group runs workshops in schools, and once a month it hosts a Sweatshop Social: "There's music, drinks, sewing machines, and fabrics," says Glenn. "We want to make it a fun atmosphere for creativity and environmentalism. The idea is to get everyone taking responsibility."

TONGUE-IN-CHIC SKIRT

DESIGNED BY Virginia Fleck   **SKILL LEVEL** Easy

Virginia created her modern version of a circle skirt as a comment on the blatant commercialism of ever-present plastic bags. The bags are meant to get attention, so no one will overlook your entrance if you wear this sassy skirt.

SIZE
Adult, made to fit

FINISHED MEASUREMENTS
Length: Approximately 27" (68.5cm)

MATERIALS
20 plastic bags in colors or designs of your choice, plus extras for patch pockets or other embellishments (The bags shouldn't be too crinkly. Those from most mall stores work well.)

3 rolls of invisible adhesive tape, ¾" (2cm) x 1,000" (25.4m)

9" (23cm) skirt zipper

Wax paper

20" (51cm) of heavy-duty Rhino Grip double-sided acrylic adhesive strip

TOOLS
Measuring tape

Hot-glue gun

Large sheet of foam core or stiff cardboard (A recycled clean pizza box would work.)

Mat knife or X-acto knife

Straightedge, such as a yardstick

Rotary cutter (can be found in most quilt supply stores)

Self-healing cutting mat

A 2" x 2" (5cm x 5cm) piece of cardboard, doubled (This gets taped to the floor and is what the point of the screw ends of your radius tool anchors into.)

A tool to mark off radius or an extra-large compass (To make this yourself, you'll need a yardstick, a 2" (5cm) screw, a hot-glue gun, and a fine-point marker.)

1. Measure yourself. This skirt is a giant circle with a hole cut in the middle for the waist. In order for the skirt to fit, you need to figure out 2 key measurements: first, the waistline, or the radius of the inside circle; and second, the hem of the skirt, or the radius of the outer circle.

To determine the size of the waistline, measure your waist. Add 1" (2.5cm) for ease and divide by 6.28. Round the results to the nearest ¼" (6mm). This will be the radius for the waist. Write it down.

2. Decide how long you want your skirt. The skirt shown is approximately 27" (68.5cm). Add this number to your waist radius number. The total equals the hem radius number. This cannot be longer than your shortest bag.

3. Make the tool to mark off a radius. Hot-glue the screw to the end of the yardstick. It should be perpendicular to the stick and the point should extend beyond the edge. Measure down your hem radius distance and hot-glue the marker in this location with the point extending beyond the edge.

4. Cut the plastic bags along the sides from top to bottom. Smooth out and lay them flat.

5. Make a wedge-shaped template. On the foam core or cardboard, outline a wedge shape, 30" (76cm) long and 10" (25.5cm) wide at the bottom that narrows to a point at the top. Cut it out with the mat knife and straight edge.

6. Lay the template over one or more layers of plastic bags placed on the cutting mat, and use it as a guide to cut out wedges with the rotary cutter. There should be 20 in all.

7. On a large, flat surface (the floor is fine), arrange the wedges in a circle with the points at the center according to your preference of color and pattern. You'll need to overlap the edges by at least ½" (13mm). Depending on the overlap, you may find that you need 1 or 2 fewer or more wedges. At this point there is no center waist hole.

8. Using invisible tape, tape all the seams on one side. Turn the circle over and tape the seams on the reverse side.

9. Place your 2" x 2" (5cm x 5cm) doubled cardboard on the floor, and tape it down with masking tape. Lay the circle of plastic over it, making sure that the cardboard is under the very center of the circle you have made.

10. Next sink the screw end of the radius tool into the cardboard, through the center of your skirt circle. Draw the hemline of your skirt. You can tack the skirt to the floor with some invisible tape to keep it from moving.

11. Use the rotary cutter to cut along the hemline. Tape both sides of the hem, and trim any excess tape off the edge.

12. Change the radius marking tool by moving and gluing the marker to the waist radius length. Place the top of the tool at the center of the circle, and mark out the waist circle. Cut it out with the rotary cutter.

13. You now have your basic skirt. Decide where you want the back, and make a 9" (23cm) cut from the waist along a seam in back. Lay the skirt facedown.

14. Lay the zipper faceup on a piece of wax paper. Cut a 10" (25.5cm) piece of the Rhino tape. Be careful, as it is *very* sticky! Place the sticky side

down along one side of the zipper. Repeat for the other side. Press the Rhino tape firmly to the fabric of the zipper. Now turn it over and trim the Rhino tape and wax paper to the edge of the zipper fabric.

15. Position the zipper along the 9" (23cm) seam. Carefully peel the wax paper off the Rhino tape, and press it along one side of the zipper cut on the plastic bag waist seam. Repeat on the other side.

16. Reinforce the waistline with invisible tape on both sides.

17. Embellish the hem with taped-on circles from other bags, as shown, or with other decorations of your choice. If you wish, you can cut out a patch pocket or two from extra bags and tape them to the front of the skirt. (It's a handy place to keep extra tape, in case you back into something sharp.)

TOYS OUT OF TRASH

LORAN SCRUGGS

EVEN AS A YOUNG CHILD, LORAN SCRUGGS wanted to make things. When she was four or five, she says, she decided that the unfolded wrappers from Smarties candies looked like little transparent wings. She fashioned an insect body, convinced her mother to give her some tape, attached the pieces, and voilà—she'd created a dragonfly. Forty years later, Loran is still making things, though these days she uses metal—recycled tin cans and bottle caps mostly—as the medium for her clever, colorful toys and sculptures.

The artist grew up in the Pacific Northwest, where her father tinkered with everything from furniture to sweaters, and her mother, a sometime ceramist, enrolled her in art classes. Loran got a sculpture degree in the late 1980s and eventually headed for New York, where she went to galleries and installations, worked on her art (including using her own red hair to create an ironic hairball sculpture), and came up with the idea for her first tin biplane.

It was "a gift for a friend who was in the army and wanted to fly planes," Loran remembers. Up to then she'd been sending

him her version of mail art, which consisted of plastic clamshell packaging that enclosed dioramas constructed from found objects. One day, looking at a plain silver soup can, something else occurred to her. She devised a pattern for a biplane and used the slot-and-tab method to put it together. "I made lots of them for Christmas ornaments and gifts," she says. "Later I added a plate with a propeller." She also produced a transportation triptych in primary colors: a red truck for land, a yellow plane for the air, and a blue tugboat for the water.

Having accumulated a collection of bottle caps, she got the idea of using those as whistle sides.

Loran had intended to stay in New York for a year, but that stretched into three, until an interest in acupuncture propelled her back to Seattle and on to Port Townsend on the Olympic Peninsula. "It's very much an arts community with a really good vibe," she says of the picturesque seaport, where she keeps up an acupuncture practice and has set up a metalwork studio in the garage of the house she shares with Mike Kennedy, a building energy efficiency consultant, who, she notes, "is a great support to my creative life and always good for a suggestion when I'm stumped on a piece."

Her workspace is filled with boxes of flattened tin cans sorted by color, cartons of scrap tin, and a shipping crate brimming with an estimated 100,000 printed bottle caps. Alternative rock music emanates from the radio and clues visitors in to the festive quality of her creations, a joyfulness imparted by the colorfully painted tin cans and her frequent visual plays on words that highlight the recycled nature of her materials.

When she returned to the West Coast, Loran continued to make toy metal trucks and airplanes, and after she read *The Fine Art of the Tin Can* by Bobby Hansson, she experimented with tiny whistles, too. "I soldered in pennies, for a penny whistle," she remembers. "I liked the pun, but the soldering was tedious." A few years later, having accumulated a collection of bottle caps, she got the idea of using *those* as the whistle sides.

She's since branched out to flowers and other 3-D toys. "I was on Etsy," she says, "and I saw a wooden elephant with wheels." She realized that she could cover it with tin and use bottle caps for wheels. The result has been a menagerie—a grayish Spectrum Olive Oil elephant, a pink Almond Roca rabbit, a coconut milk camel (with pyramids on the bottle cap wheels), and a Tiger Balm tiger—that can be grouped as "Rush Hour in the Jungle." A gift of Altoid tins led her to a series of quirky skulls.

Loran enjoys the support and encouragement of Port Townsend's active arts community, whose members save tins for her: "People like the idea of not throwing things away." She gets together regularly with knitters, jewelers, and other

D.I.Y.
Tin Envy

Loran Scruggs admits that colorful tins have been harder to come by since the last American holdouts, the Hunt's tomato can and Spam tins, went to plain undecorated metal. But there are still a few places to look for printed containers to use in creative metalwork.

- Go to secondhand stores, but only for decorative tins, not food cans.

- Look for old coffee cans.

- Shop in international food stores or in the international district of a big city. Imported food is often still packaged in painted tins.

- If you have a friend who works at a local recycling center, ask him or her to keep an eye out for these tins.

makers for crafting sessions, and the "whole town turns out for arts-oriented events like First Saturday, when the galleries are open late; the kinetic sculpture race; and the Children's Festival, with table after table of projects."

As an acupuncturist, "I'm always trying to get people to listen to themselves," Loran says, "to hear the internal voice. Meditation is being in the present, not worried about the future, not lamenting the past. Artwork is a meditation. It's about being in the moment." And she believes it's even better if it makes someone smile.

From tin to tools, Loran's workshop (opposite top) is jammed with the raw materials of her playful art, including tops from all kinds of libations (bottom).

FLEUR DE TIN CAN

DESIGNED BY Loran Scruggs   **SKILL LEVEL** Easy

Loran Scruggs began making her tin flowers about five years ago, and she says she has visions of a garden piece with several tin varieties. This one was patterned after an echinacea flower with its turned-down petals.

FINISHED MEASUREMENTS
6" x 6" (15cm x 15cm) flower; stem length as desired

MATERIALS
Tin flower template
Card stock
Colorful tin can
3' (91cm) 16-gauge rebar tie wire

TOOLS
Scissors
Can opener
Wire snips
Tin shears
Hammer
Anvil (this could be just a ½" thick piece of steel)
Scratch awl
Piece of wood
Nail
3-sided reamer
Needle-nose pliers

NOTE: Always wear safety goggles and leather or meat cutter's gloves when working with metal.

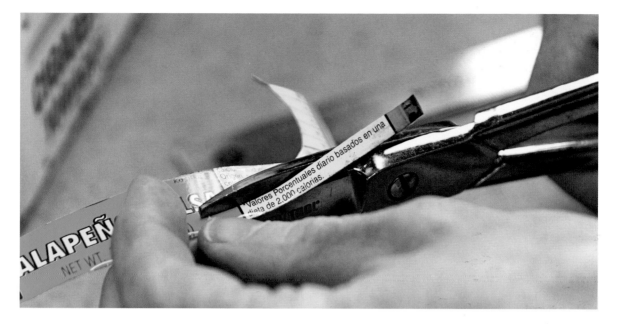

1. Copy the pattern onto card stock, and then cut it out with scissors.

2. Open up the tin can. Using a standard can opener, remove the top and bottom. Use the wire snips to cut through the two thick rings (top and bottom) and then cut them off entirely. Switch to the tin shears and cut the can down the seam. Flatten the tin as much as possible. If the can has ridges, set it onto the anvil or steel block, and use the hammer to flatten it out.

3. Trace the pattern onto the painted side of the tin using a scratch awl. The pattern is for a pair of petals connected through the center. Trace and cut out three pairs so the flower has a total of six petals.
NOTE: For a little variety, you can turn the pattern upside down to create a pair of petals that are not identical to the others.

4. Cut out the pieces using tin shears. To reduce the sharpness of the tin edges, lay each petal on the anvil and hammer the edges flat. Hammer around the whole perimeter of the piece, making sure to hit all the edges.

5. Place the petals on a piece of wood, and use a nail and hammer to make a small hole in the center of the petals, as marked. Then use the 3-sided reamer to make the hole just large enough for the wire to go through.

6. Use wire snips to cut the rebar wire to your desired length; approximately 2' to 3' (61-91cm) long. This depends on how long you would like the stem. One foot (30.5cm) will be used up in creating the ovule (the button in the center of the flower). You will be starting at the very center of the flower.

7. Use the needle-nose pliers to curl ⅛-¼" (3-6mm) of one end back about 135 degrees on itself. Use the pliers to continue crimping the end tightly onto itself to create a tight, flat spiral. Continue to curl the wire with your free hand, while using the pliers to hold the spiral flat. Keep working this way until the spiral is ½" (13mm) in diameter.

8. To create the height of the ovule, use your fingers to guide the wire under one side of the circle, creating a sort of thimble shape. Keep the wire close and tight as on the top. Coil the sides of the ovule 4 circles high.

9. To get the wire to come from the center of the bottom of the ovule, bend the wire 180 degrees and then bend it down and away from the ovule. Bend it into the ovule cap, and work with it until it comes roughly from the center.

10. Slide the petals onto the wire with the painted side facing the ovule.

11. Bend the wire over 90 degrees, and then create a circle underneath the petals, continuing to spiral as before. This circle functions to hold the petals in place.

12. Bend the wire into the center, and then bend it 90 degrees away from center and from the flower in order to create the stem.

13. Shape the petals with your fingers. Bend the petals down, and create ripples and gentle bends in the petals as desired.

TIN FLOWER TEMPLATE
ENLARGE 110%

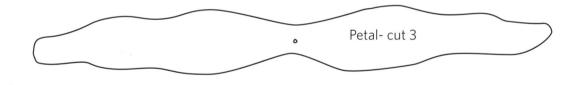

Petal- cut 3

PART V
CRAFTING A

Once upon a time the word *community* meant the people who lived next door, down the street, and around the corner. You knew your neighbors, understood their concerns, and possibly shared their background and interests, though that wasn't always the case. If anyone halfway across the country—or even the globe—had similar passions, well, you might never have known about it.

Enter the Internet and the possibility of connecting with far-flung fellow enthusiasts—in the craft world, for example—about anything from favorite materials and new techniques to worthy causes, trends, and opportunities. Knitters, in particular, were in the forefront of setting up blogs and using them to find kindred souls and build relationships. From there, it was simply another step to something like Ravelry, though who would have expected the staggering speed of that community's growth or the phenomenal breadth of its reach.

Today there are online communities serving sewers, stampers, and paper crafters, to name just a few, who may be separated geographically but are nevertheless closely united in their point of view. And craft fairs have blossomed into huge events that hopscotch around the country with a new indie spirit. The genteel juried shows of craft councils have been joined by "renegade" fairs and maker fairs that embrace technological entries and performance artists, too. Craft summits add lectures, workshops, and demonstrations designed to help independent crafters network, share information, and move to a more professional business footing.

Some community members have found that they take ideas and connections they've gotten and form new groups that better serve their needs. We now have guilds, "mafias," and collectives in particularly "crafty" towns—think Brooklyn, Boston, Austin, and Portland (Oregon)—to sponsor speakers, promote their enterprises, unite buyers and vendors, and teach crafts to new enthusiasts. Evidently getting to know distant friends may lead to getting to know your neighbors, too.

COMMUNITY

GET ORGANIZED

THE RAVELRY PHENOMENON

YOU NEVER REALLY KNOW WHERE A CREATIVE idea will lead, particularly when two people tackle a subject from different points of view. Take Ravelry, for instance. In 2004, Jessica Forbes had become passionate about the knitting she'd picked up, and she was intrigued by the challenging projects she was finding online, but keeping track of bookmarked favorites was growing ever more difficult.

Happily for fiber enthusiasts everywhere, her husband, Casey, a computer programmer, thought he might just have a way to help her organize them. No one could have predicted, however, that her interest and his approach would result in an unprecedented and powerful global online community of knitters and crocheters.

Since its launch in 2007, www.Ravelry.com has grown to one million members internationally, usually with at least 3,000 members online at a time. It boasts 15,500 groups, and 32 million posts in its forums overall, placing the site in the top fifty on the Web.

Jessica, who grew up in rural New Jersey, vaguely remembers a grandmother showing her how to knit. But she'd turned to other crafts by the time she went to the University of New Hampshire, where Casey also was a student. "He was a friend of the guys who lived next door," Jessica says, and his frequent strolls past her door hastened their romance.

After graduation, Casey's job took them to Cambridge, Massachusetts, while she commuted to Waltham. She "wanted something to do on the train," she says, "something where I could be creative and play with color. I picked up *Knitting for Dummies*, went to my local yarn store, and made a hat that was too large for any human head. That was in 2004."

> Her interest and his approach would result in an unprecedented and powerful global online community of knitters and crocheters.

When Casey told her about the knitters he saw blogging online, she launched Frecklegirl. com. In 2005, Jessica put up a screenshot on her blog and rough notes for a knitting Web site designed by Casey and asked her knitting buddies for input. "The idea is to create an encyclopedia of cool patterns and mix in

---

CLOCKWISE FROM TOP LEFT: Casey and Jessica Forbes with Boston terrier Bob; Bob "heads" to a Ravelry meet-up in New York; getting up close and personal; name tag connections; a virtual Ravelry office meeting.

Mary-Heather Cogar and the Ravelry team greet members at a Ravelry event at Yarnmarket.

blogging and other social aspects," Casey explained in the post. The enthusiastic response brought in suggestions and comments, but other responsibilities prevented the pair from developing the idea further.

"It was our 2007 New Year's resolution to really start working on it," Jessica says. By then she had left her job; Casey's work also allowed him more time to develop Ravelry. When the site went live, so many people joined that there was a lag until hosting capacity caught up with demand.

From the beginning there were certain principles as well as low-key good humor. The site would be free and inclusive. "Our idea was that anyone who blogged about a pattern or yarn could connect," says Casey. "It was important to not make people re-create what they had done.

We needed everybody's contributions, because without it, Ravelry is just an empty shell."

The pair also wanted members to be able to find creations by independent designers. "There was a disconnect," Jessica notes, "between patterns that people were blogging about and what was in magazines. We wanted people to get recognized. And as we've gone on, we try to remember what the goals were when we started, and to keep in mind the industry that we're part of. Now it's normal for companies to interact with customers online," she adds, "but we were trying to encourage that early on. Much of Ravelry's role in our industry now is to help people learn about how empowering that connection can be for [business] owners, knitters, and crocheters."

Left to right: Rooting for Ravelry; an amigurumi dragon makes an appearance.

Volunteers still handle many parts of Ravelry, from the wiki help section to administering forums. But there are also two full-time employees: Mary-Heather Cogar, who works on advertising and events from Albuquerque, and Sarah Bible, in Houston, who's responsible for community support.

In July 2009, the Forbeses moved the business out of their house and into an unprepossessing office furnished with two computers, a couch, a microwave, a water cooler, a few mementos, and space for the couple's Boston terrier, Bob. They ride their scooter to work, and talk with their team in a chat room or meet regularly through Skype. Once a month they're on the road at trade and yarn shows, retreats, parties, and store events, which can

draw as many as five hundred people at a time. "It's fun to meet people in person," Jessica says. "You have a chance to sit and talk."

There's a lot to talk about, beginning with how much the site has evolved. "I wrote the whole thing from scratch," Casey says, and it's become more complex as software and browsers have become available. "If you had showed me the site we have now and said, 'Build it,' I'd say, 'No way.'"

"The power of our community to pull people together is amazing," says Jessica. "We had the idea, and people have helped make it what it is. It's been an amazing journey."

Makers Jam

The citizens of the Ravelry world span the United States and the globe. But some famously active DIY communities are rooted in a physical town or metropolitan area, where new organizations—call them guilds, mafias, whatever you like— have sprung up to encourage, teach, and promote local crafters.

Boston already had a well-established knitting guild, when Guido Stein organized the **COMMON COD FIBER GUILD** in October 2008. But Guido, who podcasts as "It's a Purl, Man," felt that there was room for more. For one thing, the original guild met from 10 a.m. to 2 p.m. The new organization had evening get-togethers accessible to fiber enthusiasts who worked during the day, and it made a point of bringing to town speakers that Bostonians were hearing about online.

Meetings are held six times a year, with an hour set aside for lectures, demonstrations, and discussion, but no teaching. "We don't want to cut into what the yarn shops are doing," says Guido.

After a first season that concentrated on getting things running, the second season added special events, like FiberCamp. At that "unconference," Guido pointed out that no one was a rock star, meaning that a wiki type of organization and sign-up allowed participants to teach or attend sessions, according to their interests. Common Cod also promoted a Designers' Showcase, a fashion show that celebrated Boston's masters of the fiber arts.

Common Cod is "about making sure people feel a part of the group and a part of running it," says Guido—essentially fostering community and making people feel the connection.

Virtually every crafter knows **ETSY.COM** as a global online marketplace; there are 400,000 active sellers, after all, and ten times as many buyers, accounting for more than $20 million in sales a month. Etsy is also a community, however, with a home in Brooklyn and a blog—the Storque— that alerts members to virtual chats, online workshops, demonstrations, crafting "causes," seasonal handmade cavalcades, and weekly craft nights that may draw sixty or seventy people to the creative, craft-filled Etsy offices. Occasionally, there are coast-to-coast events, with contingents meeting in San Francisco, too. What's on the horizon? Perhaps Skype, so you can see and talk to each artist.

The **AUSTIN CRAFT MAFIA** may have had its roots in informal meetings between embroidery guru Jenny Hart (Sublime Stitching), DIY fashion designer Tina Sparkles, and jeweler Jennifer Perkins (Naughty Secretary Club), but since 2003 the group has morphed into a core of nine members whose influence has spread far beyond their own Texas city. Key to the organization is the fact that each of the members owns a business that does not compete with the others, allowing them to more productively

collaborate on networking, promotion, and sharing ideas—in their own words, amplifying "their individual vision through the power of the collective."

Other members of the "familia" include Susann Keohane (All Dressed Up and Shy), creator of one-of-a-kind garments; Karly Hand (Design Crisis), who does interior design and DIY home goods; Jesse Kelly-Landes of Hope and Glory Pastry; Hope Perkins (Hot Pink Pistol), a creator of vintage hand-painted purses, clothes, and art; Jenifer Nakatsu Arntson (JNA Designs), who fashions accessories; and Vickie Howell, designer, writer, and marketing consultant.

Inevitably, the buzz about the Austin Craft Mafia led to queries by artists in other cities, and in response, the group started www.CraftMafia.com as a model to establish guidelines for the use of the name and to help with advertising, publicity, and special events.

Portland, Oregon, may be home to more than half a million people, but to outsiders it sometimes seems as if all of them are artists. "Portland is the kind of city that fosters creativity," notes Cathy Pitters who runs the twice-a-year **CRAFTY WONDERLAND** fairs with Torie Nguyen. The two are half of PDX SuperCrafty—the others are Rachel O'Rourke and Susan Beal—which started with informal dinners and idea-sharing, organized as a collective to pool resources for advertising, and published a book that showcased their work, in the process highlighting the city's creative side.

Since then the SuperCrafty members have concentrated more on their own design businesses, but the Portland craft community has continued to grow, says Nguyen. The Crafty Wonderland fairs now host about two hundred local and regional vendors, and the recent Summit of Awesome, an annual three-day conference of panels, workshops, and demonstrations designed to help artists better market their work, found a large, receptive audience in the town.

Another Portland craft institution is also adapting to the evolving art scene: Jen Neitzel founded the **DIY LOUNGE** in 2006 as a place where artists in many media could teach and earn money, but the overwhelming success of the program left her little time for her own art. She's now swapped a physical location for a virtual one, putting out online video tutorials and developing "webisodes" on Portland's craft culture. "It's a way to share what's cool here with the world," Neitzel says.

D.I.Y. How to Craft a Craft Fair

Think you're ready to move from an informal craft night among friends to something a little grander? Here's a checklist of things to keep in mind, from **Kelly Rand**, program director of **Hello Craft**, a nonprofit trade organization of independent crafters and makers and the group behind the oh-so-successful Crafty Bastards show in Washington, D.C.

- Decide on the focus of the fair—diverse or targeted—for example, all jewelry. Will you take vendors on a first-come, first-served basis, or will the show be juried?

- Figure out a budget and what to charge vendors.

- Pick a location—indoors or out? Will you need permits?

- Find yourself a partner in crime. It's easier to handle all the details if there's more than one organizer.

- Involve the community to get sponsors and elicit feedback on what people want to see. Work with local businesses to make the affair a success. Remember that they can provide food options or demonstrations.

- Integrate information about the fair online with a Web site, a blog, and a vendors' showcase that allows visitors to plan their shopping in advance. And make sure the vendors also have tools to promote themselves, such as news releases to which they can add their own information.

- Promote the fair early and often to make sure you gather as large a crowd as possible.

- Round up some volunteers for the event. You (even two of you) can't do it all.

- Make sure you provide tables and chairs or make arrangements for vendors to rent them. Figure out how to feed the vendors, and on the day of the event, take care of them. For example, they may need help with transporting their merchandise.

- Make sure you have a cleanup crew.

Before you know it, you'll be planning for the next year.

CRAFTITUDE VEST

DESIGNED BY Kirsten Kapur of Through the Loops   **SKILL LEVEL** Intermediate

Kirsten Kapur has emerged on Ravelry as a gem of a knitwear designer, with fans who eagerly await her latest patterns, which combine traditional elements with contemporary shapes and textures. For this vest, she began with cables but gave it feminine touches by lengthening the body, adding shaping, and scooping the neckline.

SIZE
XS (S, M, L, XL)

FINISHED MEASUREMENTS
Bust 29 ½ (33 ½, 37 ¾, 41 ¼, 45 ½)" (75 [85, 96, 105, 115.5]cm)

MATERIALS
5 (5, 6, 7, 8) skeins Berroco Blackstone Tweed, 65% Wool, 25% Superkid Mohair, 10% Angora Rabbit Hair, 1 ¾ oz (50g), 130 yd (119m) in 2635 Wharf

TOOLS
Size U.S. 5 (3.75mm) 24" (61cm) circular needles, or two sizes smaller than size used to obtain gauge
Size U.S. 7 (4.5mm) 24" (61cm) circular needles, or size to obtain gauge
4 Stitch markers
Stitch holder or scrap yarn
Cable needle
Size U.S. 5 (3.75mm) double-pointed needles, or two sizes smaller than size used to obtain gauge
Tapestry needle

GAUGE
19 stitches and 28 rows = 4" (10cm) in stockinette stitch on larger needles

BACK

With smaller-size circular needles, cast on 72 (82, 92, 100, 110) stitches.

ROW 1: Work in k1, p1 rib for 1" (2.5cm), ending with a WS row.

Switch to larger needles.

Work in stockinette stitch until piece measures 3 (3½, 3½, 4, 4)" (7.5 [9, 9, 10, 10]cm) from the cast-on edge, ending with a RS row.

NEXT ROW (WS): P19 (21, 23, 25, 27), place marker, p34 (40, 46, 50, 56) place marker, p19 (21, 23, 25, 27).

WAIST SHAPING

NOTE: Where m1 is indicated in the instructions, simply pick up the bar between the stitches and knit it through the back loop.

DECREASE ROW (RS): Knit to 2 stitches before the marker, k2tog, slip marker, knit to the next marker, slip marker, ssk, knit to end of row.

Work 7 rows in stockinette stitch.

Repeat the last 8 rows 4 more times—62 (72, 82, 90, 100) stitches.

INCREASE ROW (RS): Knit to the marker, m1, slip marker, knit to the next marker, slip marker, m1, knit to end.

Work 7 rows in stockinette stitch.

Repeat the last 8 rows 4 more times—72 (82, 92, 100, 110) stitches.

Work until piece measures 16½ (17, 17, 17½, 17½)" (42 [43, 43, 44.5, 44.5]cm) from the cast-on edge.

ARMHOLES

Bind off 4 (5, 6, 8, 10) stitches at the beginning of the next two rows.

NEXT ROW (RS): K1, ssk, knit to the last 3 stitches, k2tog, k1.

NEXT ROW (WS): Purl.

Repeat these last two rows 4 (6, 8, 9, 9) times total—56 (60, 64, 66, 72) stitches.

Work in stockinette stitch until the armhole measures 8 (8 1/2, 9, 9½, 10)" (20.5 [21.5, 23, 24, 25.5]cm).

NEXT ROW (RS): K16 (17, 18, 19, 21) and place these 16 (17, 18, 19, 21) stitches on a holder. Bind off 24 (26, 28, 28, 30) stitches and knit to end—16 (17, 18, 19, 21) stitches remain.

LEFT SHOULDER SHAPING

ROW 1 (WS): Bind off 5 (5, 5, 5, 6) stitches, purl to end—11 (12, 13, 14, 15) stitches.

ROW 2 (RS): K1, ssk, knit to end—10 (11, 12, 13, 14) stitches.

ROW 3: Bind off 5 (5, 5, 6, 6) stitches, purl to end—5 (6, 7, 7, 8) stitches.

ROW 4: K1, ssk, knit to end—4 (5, 6, 6, 7) stitches.

Bind off remaining stitches.

RIGHT SHOULDER SHAPING

With the wrong side facing, attach yarn at the neck edge, and purl 1 row.

ROW 1 (RS): Bind off 5 (5, 5, 5, 6) stitches, knit to the last 3 stitches, k2tog, k1—10 (11, 12, 13, 14) stitches.

ROW 2 (WS): Purl.

ROW 3: Bind off 5 (5, 5, 6, 6), knit to the last 3 stitches, k2tog, k1—4 (5, 6, 6, 7) stitches.

ROW 4: Purl.

Bind off remaining stitches.

FRONT

With smaller-size needles, cast on 72 (82, 92, 100, 110) stitches.

Work in k1, p1 rib for 1" (2.5cm), ending with a

WS row.

Switch to larger needles.

NEXT ROW (RS): K4, m1, k4, m1, k10 (15, 20, 24, 29) place marker, work the next 36 stitches in Row 1 of cable chart, place marker, k10 (15, 20, 24, 29), m1, 4, m1, k4—76 (86, 96, 104, 114) stitches.

Work in stockinette stitch to the first marker, work in cable chart between markers, work in stockinette stitch to end. Continue in this manner until work measures 3 (3½, 3½, 4, 4), (7.5 [9, 9, 10, 10]cm) from the cast-on edge, ending with a RS row.

NEXT ROW (WS): P19 (21, 23, 25, 27), place marker, work 38 (44, 50, 54, 60) stitches as established, place marker, p19 (21, 23, 25, 27).

WAIST SHAPING

DECREASE ROW (RS): Knit to 2 stitches before the marker, k2tog, slip marker, work as established to the next marker, slip marker, ssk, knit to end of row.

Work 7 rows as established.

Repeat the last 8 rows 4 more times—66 (76, 86, 94, 104) stitches.

INCREASE ROW (RS): Knit to the marker, m1, slip marker, work as established to the next marker, slip marker, m1, knit to end of row.

Work 7 rows as established.

Repeat the last 8 rows 4 more times—76 (86, 96, 104, 114) stitches.

Work until piece measures 16½ (17, 17, 17½, 17½)" (42 [43, 43, 44.5, 44.5]cm) from the cast-on edge, ending with a WS row.

ARMHOLE AND NECK SHAPING

Bind off 4 (5, 6, 8, 10) stitches at the beginning of the next 2 rows.

NEXT ROW (RS): K1, ssk, work as established to

the last 3 stitches, k2tog, k1.

NEXT ROW (WS): Purl.

Repeat these last 2 rows 4 (6, 8, 9, 9) times total—60 (64, 68, 70, 76) stitches.

NEXT ROW (RS): Work 21 (22, 23, 24, 26) stitches in pattern and place these stitches on a holder for the left front. Bind off 18 (20, 22, 22, 24) stitches, work in pattern to end—21 (22, 23, 24, 26) stitches.

NEXT ROW (WS): Work in pattern.

RIGHT FRONT

NEXT ROW (RS): K1, ssk, work in pattern to end.

NEXT ROW (WS): Work in pattern.

Repeat the last 2 rows 6 more times—14 (15, 16, 17, 19) stitches.

Work as established until armhole measures 8 (8½, 9, 9½, 10)" (20.5 [21.5, 23, 24, 25.5]cm), ending with a RS row.

RIGHT SHOULDER SHAPING

NEXT ROW (WS): Bind off 5 (5, 5, 5, 6) stitches, purl to end—9 (10, 11, 12, 13) stitches.

NEXT ROW: Knit.

NEXT ROW: Bind off 5 (5, 5, 6, 6) stitches, purl to end—4 (5, 6, 6, 7) stitches.

NEXT ROW: Knit.

Bind off remaining stitches.

LEFT FRONT

Place the 21 (22, 23, 24, 26) left front stitches onto the needles. With the wrong side facing, join the yarn at the neck edge and work in pattern to end.

NEXT ROW (RS): Work in pattern to the last 3 stitches, k2tog, k1.

NEXT ROW (WS): Work in pattern.

Repeat the last 2 rows 6 more times—14 (15, 16, 17, 19) stitches.

Work as established until armhole measures 8 (8½, 9, 9½, 10)" (20.5 [21.5, 23, 24, 25.5]cm), ending with a WS row.

LEFT SHOULDER SHAPING

NEXT ROW (RS): Bind off 5 (5, 5, 5, 6) stitches, knit to end—9 (10, 11, 12, 13) stitches.

NEXT ROW: Purl.

NEXT ROW: Bind off 5 (5, 5, 6, 6) stitches, knit to end—4 (5, 6, 6, 7) stitches.

NEXT ROW: Purl.

NEXT ROW: Bind off remaining stitches.

FINISHING

Weave in all ends.

Block front and back pieces.

Sew shoulder seams.

Sew side seams.

ARMHOLE AND NECK BANDS

With double-pointed needles, beginning at the underarm seam, pick up 80 (86, 94, 102, 110) stitches around the armhole edge, work 7 rounds in k1, p1 rib. Bind off in pattern. Repeat for the other armhole.

With double-pointed needles, beginning at the right neck seam, pick up 114 (116, 120, 122, 130) stitches around the neck edge, and work 7 rounds in k1, p1 rib. Bind off in rib pattern.

Weave in ends.

LEGEND

purl
RS: purl stitch
WS: knit stitch

knit
RS: knit stitch
WS: purl stitch

c2 over 2 right
RS: sl2 to CN, hold in back. k2, k2 from CN

c2 over 2 left
RS: sl 2 to CN, hold in front. k2, k2 from CN

c2 over 2 right P
RS: sl2 to CN, hold in back. k2, p2 from CN

c2 over 2 left P
RS: sl 2 to CN, hold in front. p2, k2 from CN

c2 over 1 right P
RS: sl1 to CN, hold in back. k2, p1 from CN

c2 over 1 left P
RS: sl2 to CN, hold in front. p1, k2 from CN

6¾ (6¾, 6¾, 7, 7½)"

8 (8½, 9, 9½, 10)"

29½ (33½, 37¾, 41¼, 45½)"

25¼ (29½, 33½, 37, 41¼)"

16½ (17, 17, 17½ , 17½)"

24½ (25½, 26, 27, 27½)"

29½ (33½, 37¾, 41¼, 45½)"

CABLE PATTERN

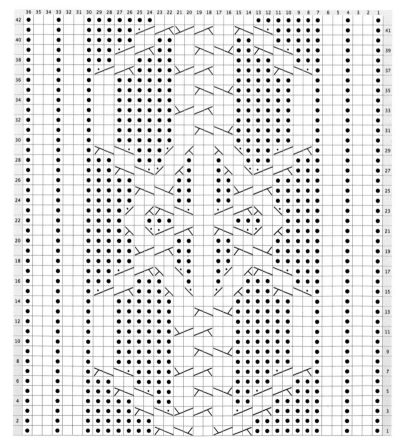

LONG DAY TO STARLIT NIGHT WRAP

DESIGNED BY Kat Coyle   **SKILL LEVEL** Intermediate

Kat Coyle, another popular Ravelry designer, created this versatile wrap. In designing it, Kat imagined a French sailor romance, in which a sad traveler makes the brave journey from stormy daytime seas to a clear starlit night. The shawl, which can also be worn as a scarf, is crafted with pima cotton garter stitch stripes, whimsical embroidery, and a gentle crochet edging.

FINISHED MEASUREMENTS
12" x 56" (30.5 x 142cm)

MATERIALS
4 balls Berroco Pure Pima, 100% Pima Cotton, 1 ¾ oz (50g), 115 yd (106m) in #2203 Oyster (MC)

1 ball Berroco Pure Pima, 100% Pima Cotton, 1 ¾ oz (50g), 115 yd (106m) in #2255 Baton Rouge (CC1)

1 ball Berroco Pure Pima, 100% Pima Cotton, 1 ¾ oz (50g), 115 yd (106m); in #2267 Blue Lagoon (CC2)

1 yd (91cm) medium-weight Natural colored 100% linen fabric

Sewing thread to match MC

1 skein of each color DMC 6 Strand Embroidery Floss, 100% cotton; unless otherwise noted

NOTE: Floss colors are sold by number only (except for Blanc); these color names are being added to make the instructions easier to follow.

Blanc (moon, stars, clouds, rain); 2 skeins
#817 red (sails)
#3811 light blue (flag)
#839 brown (ship)
#840 light brown (ropes and mast)
#3750 dark blue (ocean, moon, star outline)
#517 medium blue (ocean)
#518 medium blue (ocean)
#519 blue (ocean)

#3820 gold (sun)
#90 variegated yellow (sun)
#3808 teal (ocean)

TOOLS

Size U.S. 6 (4mm) straight needles, or size to obtain the correct gauge

Tapestry needle for weaving in yarn ends

Scissors

Straight pins

Tracing paper

Washable marker for transferring embroidery design onto fabric

Embroidery needle

Embroidery hoop

Sewing needle

Iron

Size F-5 (3.75mm) crochet hook, or size to obtain the correct gauge

GAUGE

Knitting: 21 stitches and 42 rows = 4" (10cm) in garter stitch

Crochet: 20 stitches and 9 rows = 4" (10cm) in double crochet

STITCH GUIDE

STRIPE SEQUENCE A

With MC, knit 10 rows.
With CC1, knit 2 rows.

STRIPE SEQUENCE B

With MC, knit 10 rows.
With CC2, knit 2 rows.

- -

SCARF

KNIT SECTION

NOTE: Carry the yarn not in use along the edge so you don't have to cut and tie in new yarns for every stripe. Work the knit section in garter stitch.

With MC, cast on 63 stitches.

Work Stripe Sequence A 13 times, 156 rows total.
Cut CC1.

Work Stripe Sequence B 13 times, 312 rows total from the cast-on edge. Knit 10 rows with MC.
Bind off all stitches, 322 rows total from cast-on edge.

Weave in ends.

EMBROIDERED SECTION

Prewash and dry the linen. Iron fabric.

Cut 4 pieces of linen 13½" (34.5cm) square.

With the black marking pen, trace each drawing onto tracing paper.

To transfer the traced drawing onto your fabric, use a light box, or tape the tracing paper to a light-filled window. Center your fabric over the drawing, tape down the fabric, and with a washable marking pen, trace the drawing onto the linen.

Use 3 strands of floss for the embroidery. Using an embroidery hoop will help make your stitches neat and keep your fabric from puckering.

DAY SCENE
Clouds

With Blanc, outline in stem stitch the clouds, cloud swirls, and raindrops.

Sun

With #90 (variegated yellow) and stem stitch, outline the curved line of the sun. Continue on with #90 to fill in the sun with satin stitch. Use #90 and running stitch to create radiating sun beams. Save some sunbeam area to complete with #3820 (gold).

Ship

With #839 (brown) and stem stitch, outline all the lines of the body of the ship.
With #840 (light brown) and stem stitch, outline

the lines of the ropes and mast of the ship.
With #817 (red) and stem stitch, outline the lines of the sails.
With #3811 (light blue) and satin stitch, fill in both flags.

Ocean

Working with 5 different blues and outlining the waves with the darkest color in the dips of the waves and the lightest color on the crest of the waves helps to give the ocean depth.
With #3750 (dark blue) and stem stitch, outline the dips of the last line of waves.
With # 3808 (teal), outline the dips of the rest of the waves.
With #517 (medium blue), working close to the other stitches, outline the last line of waves.
With #518 (blue), working close to the other stitches, outline the rest of the waves.
With #519 (blue), working close to the other stitches, outline the crest of each wave.

NIGHT SCENE
Ship

Work as the Day Scene except for the flags: With #3811 (light blue) and stem stitch, outline both flags, fill in the left-hand flag with stem stitch, make an X with straight stitch on the right-hand flag.

Clouds, Moon, and Stars

With Blanc and stem stitch, outline the moon, clouds, the lines connecting the clouds, and the large star to the right of the moon.
With Blanc, fill in the moon with satin stitch.
With Blanc and French knots create the stars.
With Blanc and straight stitches, create medium-sized stars. The straight stitches are worked in

crisscrossing star shapes.

With #517 (medium blue) and stem stitch, working inside the white lines, outline the cloud beneath the moon. Outline the cloud to the left of the moon, working on the outside of the white lines. Continue to follow the lines connecting to the next cloud, and outline on the inside of the white lines.

With #3750 (dark blue) and stem stitch, working outside the white lines, outline the large star the lower cloud, and the moon. Working on the inside of the white lines, outline the cloud to the left of the moon.

Ocean

Work as the Day Scene but using 4 blues instead of 5, eliminating #3808 teal.

When embroidery is complete, gently hand-wash the fabric in cool, sudsy water. Let the fabric sit in water until the pen drawing has been rinsed out. Rinse the soap out, gently squeeze excess water from the fabric, between towels, and lay it flat to dry.

To iron, place embroidery facedown on a fluffy towel and press gently. Then, with right sides together (one embroidered side, and one plain back side), baste pieces of fabric together along the left and right sides with a ⅝" (16mm) seam allowance. Leave the top and bottom edges unsewn. Pin to the knit fabric to check that the width is correct. Hand- or machine-sew pieces together along each vertical side. Press seams (trim excess fabric at the seam, as needed). Turn down ⅝" (16mm) at top and bottom edges and press. Turn right-side out. Pin the fabric to knit edges so that the knit fits between the front and back of the linen fabric. With sewing thread and needle, neatly hand sew to the knitting.

CROCHET SECTION (MAKE 2)

With MC and crochet hook, chain 63.

ROW 1: Double crochet into 4th chain from hook, double crochet in each chain. You'll have 60 double crochet including the turning chain.

ROW 2: Turn work, chain 4 (counts as first double crochet and chain 1), *skip 1 double crochet, double crochet in following double crochet, chain 1; repeat from *; end with a double crochet.

ROW 3: Turn work, chain 1 (counts as first single crochet), * single crochet in chain-1 space, single crochet in next double crochet; repeat from *; end with a single crochet.

Cut yarn, weave in end.

Wet-block the crocheted pieces, pinning them to size. This will open up the pattern to help it lay flat.

Pin crochet edging between linen panels so that the row of single crochet at the top of the edging fits between the front and back of the linen fabric. With sewing thread and needle, neatly hand-sew in place.

ENLARGE ALL
TEMPLATES
150%

LOUNGE ACT CARDIGAN

DESIGNED BY Ann Weaver   **SKILL LEVEL** Intermediate

Ann Weaver says this piece resembles what Kurt Cobain wore in the video for Nirvana's hit song "Smells Like Teen Spirit." The song and the video made such a strong impression on her when it came out that, nineteen years later, she realized she wanted a garment just like that one, only as a cardigan—so she made one. Sized and styled for both men and women, with optional waist shaping and left- or right-facing button-band options, this thrift-store, grunge-inspired design is spruced up here so it can flatter all ages, sizes, and tastes.

SIZE
XS (S, M, L, XL)

FINISHED MEASUREMENTS
Chest: 35 ½ (37 ½, 43 ½, 48 ¾, 53)" (90 [95, 110.5, 124, 134.5]cm), buttoned.

The finished measurement includes approximately 4" (10cm) of positive ease.

Length: 22 ½ (23, 25 ¾, 27, 29 ¾)" (57 [58.5, 65.5, 68.5, 75.5]cm)

MATERIALS
3 (3, 4, 4, 5) skeins Berroco Ultra Alpaca yarn, 50% Super Fine Alpaca, 50% Merino Wool, 3 ½ oz (100g), 215 yd (198m); Color A #6225 Masa

2 (2, 3, 3, 3) skeins Berroco Ultra Alpaca yarn, 50% Super Fine Alpaca, 50% Merino Wool, 3 ½ oz (100g), 215 yd (198m); Color B #6253 Dijon

2 (2, 2, 2, 3) skeins Berroco Ultra Alpaca, 50% Super Fine Alpaca, 50% Merino Wool, 3 ½ oz (100g), 215 yd (198m); Color C #6289 Charcoal Mix

[4 MEDIUM]

6 buttons, approximately 1" (2.5cm) diameter

TOOLS
Size U.S. 7 (4.5mm) 32" (81cm) circular needle or size needed to obtain gauge

Size U.S. 7 (4.5mm) 16" (40.5cm) circular needle or size needed to obtain gauge

10 stitch markers (4 in a different color than the other 6)

2 stitch holders or scrap yarn

Tapestry needle

Sewing needle and matching thread

GAUGE

20 stitches and 28 rows = 4" (10cm) in stockinette stitch
To save time, take time to check gauge.

NOTE: This sweater is worked in one piece from the top down. Markers are placed to distinguish the button bands, fronts, sleeves, and back sections.

STITCH GUIDE

BUTTONHOLE FOR MAN'S CARDIGAN

ROW 1 (RS): Work the first 4 stitches of the row in pattern, bind off the next 2 stitches, work in pattern to end.

ROW 2 (WS): Work in pattern to the bound-off stitches in the previous row. Cast on 2 stitches over the bound-off stitches, work in pattern to end.

BUTTONHOLE FOR WOMAN'S CARDIGAN

ROW 1 (RS): Work in pattern to the last 6 stitches of the row, bind off the next 2 stitches, work in pattern to end.

ROW 2 (WS): Work the first 4 stitches of the row in pattern, cast on 2 stitches over the bound off stitches in the previous row, work in pattern to end.

STRIPE SEQUENCE

NOTE: Work the stripe sequence entirely in stockinette stitch, with the exception of the button bands at the ends of each row.

With A, work until stripe measures 4 (4, 4 ½, 4 ½, 5)" (10 [10, 11.5, 11.5, 12.5]cm). Work buttonhole (as instructed above) when stripe measures 3 (3, 3, 3, 4)" (7.5 [7.5, 7.5, 7.5, 10] cm).

Cut A and join C. Work 2 rows.

Cut C and join B. Work 11 (11, 13, 13, 15) rows.

Cut B and join C. Work 2 rows.

Cut C and join B. Work 11 (11, 13, 13, 15) rows. Work buttonhole (as instructed above) starting on Row 5 (5, 5, 5, 6) or the next row, if this is a wrong side row.

Cut B and join C. Work 2 rows.

The stripe sequence is worked twice on the cardigan body and the cardigan sleeves. Since 2 buttonholes are created during each stripe sequence, a total of 4 buttonholes will be created during striping. After these stripe repetitions are completed, the body of the cardigan is finished in A and the sleeves are finished in C.

YOKE

With 32" (81cm) circular needle and A, cast on 10 front band stitches, place marker, cast on 14 (14, 16, 16, 18) front stitches, place marker, cast on 1 stitch, place marker, cast on 12 (12, 12, 14, 14) sleeve stitches, place marker, cast on 1 stitch, place marker, cast on 29 (31, 33, 35, 37) back stitches, place marker, cast on 1 stitch, place marker, cast on 12 (12, 12, 14, 14) sleeve stitches, place marker, cast on 1 stitch, place marker, cast on 14 (14, 16, 16, 18) front stitches, place marker, cast on 10 stitches—105 (107, 113, 119, 125) stitches total.

Work in k1, p1 rib for 1" (2.5cm), ending with a WS row. Work buttonhole over the next 2 rows. Continue in k1, p1 rib until piece measures 2" (5cm) from the cast-on edge.

BEGIN TO WORK STRIPE SEQUENCE

SET-UP ROW (RS): Work 10 sts in k1, p1 rib for the front band, slip marker, k to last marker working k2tog at center back, slip marker, work 10 sts in k1, p1 rib for the front band.

Work 1 WS row, and then begin raglan increases as follows:

ROW 1 (RS): Work to the second marker, *make 1 Right (m1R), slip marker, k1, slip marker, make 1 Left (m1L), work to the next marker*; repeat from * to * 3 more times, work to end.

ROW 2 (WS): Work in pattern.

Work Rows 1 and 2, above, 26 (28, 30, 29, 33) times total.

CONTINUE TO WORK RAGLAN INCREASES FOR YOUR SIZE AS FOLLOWS:

ROW 1 (RS): Work to the second marker, *m1R, slip marker, k1, slip marker, m1L, work to the next marker*, repeat from * to * 3 more times, work to end.

ROW 2 (WS): Work to the second marker, *m1R, slip marker, p1, slip marker, m1L, work to the next marker*: repeat from * to * 3 more times, work to end.

Work Rows 1 and 2, above, 0 (0, 0, 1, 1) times, then repeat Row 1 0 (0, 0, 1, 1) additional time total—312 (330, 352, 374, 412) stitches.

Continue to work raglan increases for your size as follows, increasing only the fronts and back of the cardigan and working even across the sleeve stitches:

Next Row: Work to the 2nd marker, m1R, work to the 5th marker, slip marker, m1L, work to the next marker, m1R, work to the 9th marker, m1L, slip marker, work to end.

Work this row 0 (0, 4, 6, 6) times total.

NOTE: From now on, the front stitch totals will include the front bands. However, the front band stitch markers should be left in place as a reminder of where the pattern changes.

50 (52, 60, 64, 70) left front stitches; 1 border stitch; 64 (68, 72, 78, 86) left sleeve stitches; 1 border stitch; 80 (86, 100, 110, 120) back stitches; 1 border stitch; 64 (68, 72, 78, 86) right sleeve stitches; 1 border stitch; 50 (52, 60, 64, 70) right front stitches.

DIVIDE BODY FROM SLEEVES

Work the first 50 (52, 60, 64, 70) stitches in pattern, to the 2nd marker. Place the next 66 (70, 74, 80, 88) stitches on a stitch holder, removing 2nd, 3rd, 4th, and 5th markers. Cast on 5 (5, 5, 9, 9) underarm stitches, placing marker after the 3rd (3rd, 3rd, 5th, 5th) stitch to mark the side seam. Work the next 80 (86, 100, 110, 120) stitches, to the 6th marker. Place the next 66 (70, 74, 80, 88) stitches on a stitch holder or length

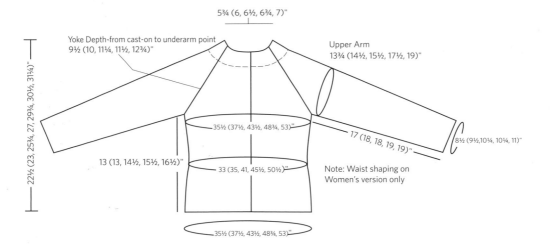

5¾ (6, 6½, 6¾, 7)"

Yoke Depth–from cast-on to underarm point
9½ (10, 11¼, 11½, 12¾)"

Upper Arm
13¾ (14½, 15½, 17½, 19)"

22½ (23, 25¾, 27, 29¾, 30½, 31¼)"

35½ (37½, 43½, 48¾, 53)"

17 (18, 18, 19, 19)"

8½ (9½,10¼, 10¼, 11)"

13 (13, 14½, 15½, 16½)"

33 (35, 41, 45½, 50½)"

Note: Waist shaping on
Women's version only

35½ (37½, 43½, 48¾, 53)"

of waste yarn, removing the 6th, 7th, 8th, and 9th markers. Cast on 5 (5, 5, 9, 9) underarm stitches, placing the marker after the 2nd (2nd, 2nd, 4th, 4th) stitch to mark the side seam. Work the last 50 (52, 60, 64, 70) stitches in pattern—190 (200, 230, 256, 278) stitches.

For MAN'S version, skip the waist-shaping instructions and continue where indicated.

For WOMAN'S version only work waist shaping with body darts as follows:

NOTE: Remember to work Stripe Sequence, with buttonholes, at instructed intervals, while working waist shaping.

Work body in pattern until piece measures 13 (13, 13½, 14, 14½)" (33 [33, 34.5, 35.5, 37]cm) from the cast-on edge. Using contrasting markers, place markers 30 (32, 35, 37, 40) stitches from each end, and on the back, 22 (22, 27, 30, 34) stitches from each side marker. These will be referred to as the "body dart markers."

On the next right side row, work to the 2nd marker, *slip, slip, knit (ssk), slip marker, k2tog, work to the next body dart marker: repeat from * 3 more times, then work in pattern to end. Work 7 rows in pattern with no shaping.

Repeat the previous 8 rows twice more for a total of 3 decrease rows. Work an additional 7 rows in pattern with no shaping.

On the next right side row, work to the 2nd marker, *m1R, slip marker, k1, m1L, work to the next body dart marker: repeat from * 3 more times, then work in pattern to end. Work 7 rows in pattern with no shaping.

Repeat the previous 8 rows twice more for a total of 3 increase rows.

Man's version: Resume here.
Woman's version: Continue here.

Complete the stripe sequence on the body, remembering to work buttonholes at instructed intervals. Cut C, and join A. With A, work until piece measures 20½ (21, 23½, 25, 26½)" (52 [53.5, 59.5, 63.5, 67.5]cm), or 2" (5cm) short of desired length, from cast-on edge, ending with a WS row. Make sure to work buttonhole when color A segment measures 3 (3, 3, 3, 4)" (7.5 [7.5, 7.5, 7.5, 10]cm).

Work in k1, p1 rib for 2" (5cm).

Bind off loosely.

SLEEVES

Place 66 (70, 74, 80, 88) sleeve stitches onto the 16" (40.5cm) circular needle. Join the color appropriate to continue the stripe sequence on the sleeve. Work the sleeve stitches and pick up and knit 5 (5, 5, 9, 9) stitches from the underarm cast-on, placing a marker after the 3rd (3rd, 3rd, 5th, 5th) picked-up stitch to mark the underarm seam and the beginning of round. Join to work in the round—71 (75, 79, 89, 97) stitches.

NOTE: When you have finished the second Stripe Sequence, work the remainder of the sleeve in C. Work even until the sleeve measures 4" (10cm) from the underarm.

NEXT ROUND: K2tog, work to 2 stitches before the marker, ssk.

Work 5 (5, 5, 4, 3, 3, 3) rounds even.

Work these 6 (6, 6, 5, 4) rounds 14 (14, 14, 19, 21) times total—43 (47, 51, 51, 55) stitches.

NEXT ROUND: K2tog, work to end—42 (46, 50, 50, 54) stitches.

Work additional rounds with no shaping until sleeve measures measures 15" (16, 16, 17, 17) (38 [40.5, 40.5, 43, 43]cm) or 2" (5cm) less than desired length.

Work in k1, p1 rib for 2" (5cm). Bind off loosely. Repeat for the second sleeve.

FINISHING

Weave in ends.

Before sewing on buttons, steam- or wet-block cardigan to measurements. Overlap the band with buttonholes over the band without buttonholes, and mark the appropriate places for the buttons.

Using the sewing needle and matching thread, sew on buttons. Wear and enjoy!

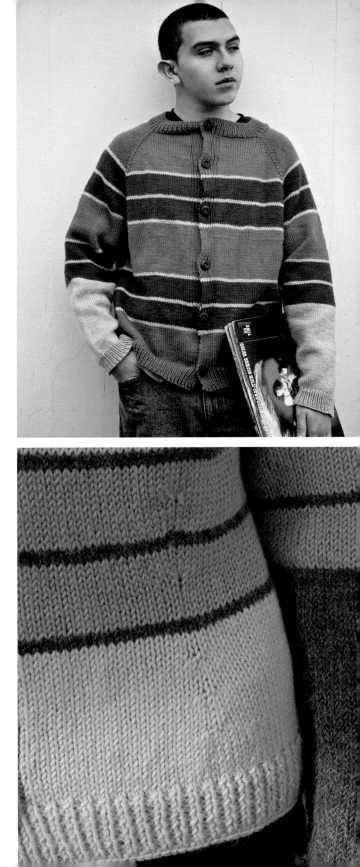

HOW TO GET CRAFTING

ARTISTS, PATTERNS, PROJECTS, STORIES, AND photographs—they're interesting to read, fun to look at, and inspiring to think about. But in the end what appears in these pages is also meant to move you to action.

How to begin?

Whether you want to learn a new craft or sharpen your skills, start with your local craft, quilting, or yarn store. Many offer classes for people at all levels, from basics to specialized projects or techniques. Look for open studio hours or sit-and-knit times, these social settings are a good way to meet people who can pass along tips and help you improve your crafting.

Try online tutorials, on YouTube or craft community sites. You'll find videos that teach everything from how to do a kitchener stitch for your hand-knit sock to how to promote your Web site. You may want to sign up for paid online classes, if no actual classes are available locally or they don't fit your schedule.

Become active in a craft community. Some of the biggest and most popular are the Etsy forums, which cover all kinds of media, or Ravelry for fiber-oriented folks. There's also Knitter's Review, an early online community. Flickr, though it began as a way to share photos, increasingly hosts groups interested in a specific craft, like embroidery, or even a certain kind of embroidery.

Follow the blogs of crafters and artists whose work you admire, and check out *their* blogrolls to widen the scope of your interests. Read craft magazines. The grandmother of online magazines, Knitty.com, has a repertoire of fresh new patterns and an archive of clear, useful instructions. Makezine.com and Craftzine.com are interesting online publications from the folks behind *Make* magazine.

Sometimes it's good to get your craft fix away from home. If you're traveling to New York (well, Brooklyn), Etsy hosts lively monthly craft nights in its offices. The Storque, Esty's blog, posts all the details. Maker Faires and Renegade Craft Fairs are a movable feast of workshops, demonstrations, and craft vendors that take place in various cities around the United States. ArtFest is an annual Port Townsend, Washington, crafters' get-together, while Boston has held several FiberCamps, wiki-organized "unconferences."

If you're truly bitten by the DIY bug and are starting to think about making crafts your life's work, don't quit your day job right away. But do take advantage of the resources, networks, and marketing venues for would-be entrepreneurs. The Summit of Awesome is an annual three-day series of panels, workshops, and demonstrations sponsored by Hello Craft, a nonprofit trade organization dedicated to advancing crafters in the DIY movement.

Etsy, of course, has revolutionized marketing for all craft vendors, making it possible to test the marketplace and get your feet wet with very little investment of time and money. With a few photos and the time to put together a template, you can open your own shop.

KNITTING ABBREVIATIONS AND YARN WEIGHT CHART

ONLINE RESOURCES ARE INVALUABLE IN providing knitting help. Both www.knittinghelp.com and www.youtube.com provide some great videos and simply doing a search of knitting terms will lead to a wealth of information.

CN: Cable needle

K: Knit

K2TOG: Knit two together

KFB: Knit in the front and back of the next stitch

KNITWISE: Insert the right needle into the front of a stitch from left to right.

M1: Make 1 stitch

M1L: Make 1 left

M1R: Make 1 right

P: Purl

PM: Place marker

PURLWISE: Insert right needle into the front of a stitch from right to left

RS: Right side

SL: Slip

SSK: Slip, slip, knit. Slip 2 stitches separately knitwise, then insert the left needle into the front of these 2 stitches and knit them together.

WS: Wrong side

WYIF: With yarn in front

YARN WEIGHT CHART

Type of Yarns in Category	FINGERING 10-COUNT CROCHET THREAD — 0 — LACE	SOCK, FINGER-ING, BABY 10-COUNT — 1 — SUPER FINE	SPORT, BABY — 2 — FINE	DK, LIGHT WORSTED — 3 — LIGHT	WORSTED, AFGHAN, ARAN — 4 — MEDIUM	CHUNKY, CRAFT, RUG — 5 — BULKY	BULKY, ROVING — 6 — SUPER BULKY
Knit Gauge Range* in Stockinette Stitch to 4 inches	33–40**sts	27–32 sts	23–26 sts	21–24 sts	16–20 sts	12–15 sts	6–11 sts
Recommended Needle in Metric Size Range	1.5–2.25mm	2.25–3.25mm	3.25–3.75mm	3.75–4.5mm	4.5–5.5mm	5.5–8mm	8 mm and larger
Recommended Needle U.S. Size Range	000–1	1–3	3–5	5–7	7–9	9–11	11 and larger
Crochet Gauge* Ranges in Single Crochet to 4 inch	32–42 double crochets**	21–32 sts	16–20 sts	12–17 sts	11–14 sts	8–11 sts	5–9 sts
Recommended Hook in Metric Size Range Stitch to 4 inches	Steel*** 1.6–1.4mm	2.25–3.5mm	3.5–4.5mm	4.5–5.5mm	5.5–6.5mm	6.5–9mm	9mm and larger
Hook U.S. Size Range	Steel*** 6, 7, 8 Regular hook B-1	B-1 to E-4	E-4 to 7	7 to I-9	I-9 to K-10½	K-10½ to M-13	M-13 and larger

* GUIDELINES ONLY: The chart reflects the most commonly used gauges and needle or hook sizes for specific yarn categories.

** Lace weight yarns are usually knitted or crocheted on larger needles and hooks to create lacy, openwork patterns. Accordingly, a gauge range is difficult to determine. Always follow the gauge stated in your pattern.

*** Steel crochet hooks are sized differently from regular hooks—the higher the number, the smaller the hook, which is the reverse of regular hook sizing

SUGGESTED READING AND OTHER RESOURCES

Knitting and Crochet

Brown, Larissa Golden, and Martin John Brown. *Knitalong: Celebrating the Tradition of Knitting Together*. New York: Stewart Tabori & Chang, 2008.

Budd, Ann. *Knitting Green: Conversations and Planet Friendly Projects*. Loveland, Colorado: Interweave Press, 2010.

Christiansen, Betty, and Kiriko Shirobayashi. *Knitting for Peace: Make the World a Better Place One Stitch at Time*. New York: Stewart Tabori & Chang, 2006.

Eaton, Jan. *200 Crochet Blocks for Blankets, Throws and Afghans*. Loveland, Colorado: Interweave Press, 2004.

Eckman, Edie. *Beyond-the-Square Crochet Motifs: 144 Circles, Hexagons, Triangles, Squares, and Other Unexpected Shapes*. North Adams, Massachusetts: Storey Publishing, 2008.

Gardiner, Kay, and Ann Shayne. *Mason-Dixon Knitting: The Curious Knitter's Guide: Stories, Patterns, Advice, Opinions, Questions, Answers, Jokes, and Pictures*. New York: Potter Craft, 2006.

___. *Mason-Dixon Knitting Outside the Lines: Patterns, Stories, Pictures, True Confessions, Tricky Bits, Whole New Worlds, and Familiar Ones, Too*. New York: Potter Craft, 2008.

Greer, Betsy. *Knitting for Good!: A Guide to Creating Personal, Social, and Political Change Stitch by Stitch*. Boston: Trumpeter, 2008.

Gschwandtner, Sabrina. *KnitKnit: Profiles and Projects from Knitting's New Wave*. New York: Stewart Tabori & Chang, 2007.

Holetz, Julie Armstrong. *Uncommon Crochet: Twenty-Five Projects Made from Natural Yarns and Alternative Fibers*. Berkeley, California: Ten Speed Press, 2008.

Moore, Mandy, and Leanne Prain. *Yarn Bombing: The Art of Crochet and Knit Graffiti*. Vancouver, British Columbia: Arsenal Pulp Press, 2009.

McYarnpants, Stitchy, and Caro Sheridan. *Knitting It Old School: 43 Vintage-Inspired Patterns*. Hoboken, New Jersey: Wiley, 2010.

Okey, Shannon. *How to Knit in the Woods: 20 Projects for the Great Outdoors*. Seattle: Skipstone, 2008.

___. *The Knitgrrl Guide to Professional Knitwear Design: How to Keep Your Knits About You*. Lakewood, Ohio: Cooperative Press, 2010.

Parkes, Clara. *The Knitter's Book of Yarn*. New York: Potter Craft, 2007

___. *The Knitter's Book of Wool*. New York: Potter Craft, 2009.

Stoller, Debbie. *Stitch 'n Bitch: The Knitter's Handbook*. New York: Workman Publishing, 2003.

___. *Stitch 'n Bitch Nation*. New York: Workman Publishing, 2004.

___. *Stitch 'n Bitch Crochet: The Happy Hooker*. New York: Workman Publishing 2006.

Turjoman, Julie. *Brave New Knits: 26 Projects and Personalities from the Knitting Blogosphere*. Emmaus, Pennsylvania: Rodale, 2010.

Werker, Kim. *Crochet Me*. Loveland, Colorado: Interweave Press, 2007.

___. *Crocheted Gifts Book*. Loveland Colorado: Interweave Press, 2009.

Quilting and Sewing

Artise, Bridgett, and Jen Karetnick. *Born-Again Vintage: 25 Ways to Deconstruct, Reinvent, and Recycle Your Wardrobe*. New York: Potter Craft, 2008.

Bell, Katherine. *Quilting for Peace: Make the World a Better Place One Stitch at a Time*. New York: Stewart Tabori & Chang, 2009

ffrench, Crispina. *The Sweater Chop Shop: Sewing One-of-a-Kind Creations from Recycled Sweaters*. North Adams, Massachusetts: Storey Publishing, 2009.

Freeman, Roland L. *A Communion of the Spirits: African-American Quilters, Preservers, and Their Stories*. Nashville, Tennessee: Rutledge Hill Press, 1996.

Geisel, EllynAnne. *The Apron Book: Making, Wearing, and Sharing a Bit of Cloth and Comfort*. Kansas City, Missouri: Andrews McMeel Publishing, 2006.

___. *The Kitchen Linens Book: Using, Sharing, and Cherishing the Fabrics of Our Daily Lives*. Kansas City, Missouri: Andrews McMeel Publishing, 2009.

Hart, Jenny. *Sublime Stitching: Hundreds of Hip Embroidery Patterns and How-to*. San Francisco: Chronicle Books, 2006.

___. *Embroidered Effects: Projects and Patterns to Inspire Your Stitching*. San Francisco: Chronicle Books, 2009.

Karol, Amy. *Bend-the-Rules Sewing: The Essential Guide to a Whole New Way to Sew*. New York: Potter Craft, 2007.

___. *Bend the Rules with Fabric: Fun Sewing Projects with Stencils, Stamps, Dye, Photo Transfers, Silk Screening, and More*. New York: Random House, 2009.

Ketteler, Judi. *Sew Retro: 25 Vintage-Inspired Projects for the Modern Girl & A Stylish History of the Sewing Revolution*. Minneapolis, Minnesota: Voyageur Press, 2010.

Mazloomi, Carolyn. *Spirits of the Cloth: Contemporary African American Quilts.* New York: Clarkson Potter, 1998.

___ . *Textural Rhythms: Quilting the Jazz Tradition.* West Chester, Ohio: Paper Moon Publishing, 2007.

___ . *Journey of Hope: Quilts Inspired by President Barack Obama.* Minneapolis, Minnesota: MBI Publishing, 2010.

Sparkles, Tina. *Little Green Dresses: 50 Original Patterns for Repurposed Dresses, Tops, Skirts, More.* Newton, Connecticut: Taunton Press, 2010.

Teufel, Linda Chang. *Quilting Party: Group Quilting for Celebration, Commemoration & Charity.* Worthington, Ohio: Dragon Threads, 2008.

Paper, Metalcraft, and Miscellaneous

Blank, Harrod. *Art Cars.* New York: Lark Books, 2002.

Hansson, Bobby. *The Fine Art of the Tin Can: Techniques & Inspirations.* New York, Lark Books, 2004.

McYarnpants, Stitchy. *The Museum of Kitschy Stitches Book.* Philadelphia: Quirk Books, 2006.

Shay, Bee. *Collage Lab: Experiments, Investigations, and Exploratory Projects (Lab Series).* Beverly, Massachusetts: Quarry Books, 2010.

The DIY Movement

Chapin, Kari. *The Handmade Marketplace: How to Sell Your Crafts Locally, Globally, and On-Line.* North Adams, Massachusetts: Storey Publishing, 2010.

Frauenfelder, Mark. *Made by Hand.* New York: Portfolio, 2010.

Howell, Vickie. *Craft Corps: Celebrating the Creative Community One Story at a Time.* New York: Lark Books, 2010.

Levine, Faythe, and Cortney Heimerl. *Handmade Nation: The Rise of DIY, Art, Craft, and Design.* New York: Princeton Architectural Press, 2008.

YARN RESOURCES

The yarns that are included in the projects in this book are widely available in yarn stores and online. If you have any trouble finding them, however, please contact the yarn companies themselves to locate distributors in your area.

Berroco: 508-278-2527; www.berroco.com

Brown Sheep Company: 800-826-9136; www.brownsheep.com

Cascade Yarns: www.cascadeyarns.com

Louet: 800-897-6444; www.louet.com

Noro: Knitting Fever International, 516-546-3600; www.knittingfever.com

The Schaefer Yarn Company: 607-532-9452; www.schaeferyarn.com

WEB RESOURCES

The following list refers to links for crafters, materials, and other information in this book.

Knit Bombing—The JafaGirls

The JafaGirls Web site is www.Jafagirls.wordpress.com.

Robyn Love blogs about her textile projects at www.robynlove.com.

You can see Carol Hummel's provocative portfolio at www.carolhummel.com.

Follow Jennifer Marsh's projects at www.internationalfibercollaborative.com.

Quilts with a Message—Carolyn Mazloomi

Carolyn Mazloomi's Web site is www.carolynmazloomi.com.

A selection of Roland Freeman's photos can be viewed at www.tgcd.org.

Gwendolyn Magee's Web site is www.gwenmagee.com.

Find out more about Lauren Cross's film at www.skinquiltproject.com.

A Knitted Spotlight on Endangered Species—Ruth Marshall

Ruth Marshall's Web site is www.ruthmarshall.com.

To find out more about where the Coral Reef Project will be on exhibit, for information about hyperbolic crochet workshops, or tips on how to start your own satellite reef, go to www.crochetcoralreef.org.

To see a gallery of Laurel Roth's work, go to www.loloro.com.

Artist Trading Cards—Bee Shay

Bee Shay's Web site is www.Beeshay.typepad.com.

The *ATC Quarterly*, based in Ontario, Canada, is a magazine devoted to traders, groups, and cards, and invites submissions. Find out more at www.atcquarterly.com.

A community-based Web site, ATCs for All, also trades cards and other forms of mail art in many media. Look it up at www.atcsforall.com.

There's more of an emphasis on person-to-person trading, which is considered a collaborative cultural performance, at Artist Trading Cards. For a list of events and other information, go to www.artist-trading-cards.ch/index.html.

Knitting Is Political–Lisa Anne Auerbach

Lisa Anne Auerbach's Web site is www.lisaanneauerbach.com.

Clara Parkes writes about yarn regularly at the weekly online magazine www.knittersreveiew.com.

Not Your Grandmother's Embroidery–Jenny Hart

Jenny Hart's Web sites are www.jennyhart.net and www.sublimestitching.com.

Shannon Okey's lively blog is at www.knitgrrl.com.

See examples of Chawne Kimber's embroidery at www.flickr.com/photos/cauchycomplete.

Paul Nosa's solar-powered sewing machine embroidery is on view at www.pnosa.com.

A New Take on Old Domestic Arts–Catherine Clark and Katie Metzger

The Web site for Brooklyn General Store is www.brooklyngeneral.com.

EllynAnn Geisel writes about aprons and other vintage linens on her Web site, www.apronmemories.com.

Return of the Granny Square–Ellen Bloom

Ellen Bloom blogs at www.ellenbloom.blogspot.com.

Follow Kim Werker's crochet comments and projects at www.kimwerker.com.

See Regina Rioux Gonzalez's crocheted creatures at www.monstercrochet.com.

Knitters United–The Red Scarf Project

Find out more about the Orphan Foundation of America and the Red Scarf Project at www.orphan.org/index.php?id=40 or at www.nownormaknits2.typepad.com/red_scarf_project_2008/

The Mitten Project at the Yarnery is publicized on the shop's Web site, www.yarnery.com/index.php?id=17.

For more about the Nest, look up www.nestmaine.blogspot.com.

If you're in the Washington, D.C., area and want to make sure a charity exists, or to find out what items it's currently looking for, go to Knitters and Crocheters Care at www.knitters-and-crocheters-care.blogspot.com.

The current needs and due dates for afghans for Afghans projects are listed at www.afghansforafghans.org.

For more information about the AIDS quilt—including a schedule of upcoming exhibitions—log on to www.aidsquilt.org.

Read more about Christmas at Sea at www.seamenschurch.org/christmas-at-sea

Follow the Mother Bear Project at www.motherbearproject.org.

Read more about the Quilts of Valor at www.qovf.org.

Ann Shayne and Kay Gardiner blog about knitting (and so many other things) at www.masondixonknitting.com.

Mary Lou Egan's Web site is www.mlegan.com.

Recycled Chic–Crispina ffrench

Crispina ffrench's Web site is www.crispina.com.

Find out more about B. Artise's work at www.b-artise.com.

You can see Natalie Chanin's line of products at www.alabamachanin.com.

The full range of BeSweet yarns and accessories are on view at www.besweetproducts.com.

One Word: Plastic–Virginia Fleck

Virginia Fleck's Web site is www.virginiafleck.com.

To find out about Bags for the People, go to www.bagsforthepeople.org.

Toys Out of Trash–Loran Scruggs

Loran Scruggs' work is at www.etsy.com/shop/loranscruggs.

Get Organized–The Ravelry Phenomenon

To find out more about Ravelry or to join, go to www.ravelry.com.

More information about the DIY communities and craft mafia in Makers Jam can be found at each group's Web site: www.commoncod.com, www.etsy.com/storque, www.austincraftmafia.com, www.craftmafia.com, www.craftywonderland.com, and www.diylounge.com.

Look up Kirsten Kapur's designs at www.throughtheloops.typepad.com.

Kat Coyle blogs at www.katcoyle.com.

See Ann Weaver's work at www.weaverknits.blogspot.com.

How to Get Crafting

For craft fairs and craft nights, look up:

www.etsy.com/storque

www.makerfaire.com

www.renegadecraft.com

www.teeshaslandofodd.com/artfest/classes.html

www.hellocraft.com

ACKNOWLEDGMENTS

THIS BOOK HAD ITS GENESIS IN GALE'S BROAD interest in crafting—even macaroni art, she has said—and her widespread network of imaginative knitters, crocheters, crafters, makers, artists, and artisans. As we researched further and narrowed our wish list of people and work to concentrate on, we're grateful to have found profile subjects and designers who were generous with the time it took to be interviewed, to be photographed, and to create something new.

We're also thankful for the indispensable contributions of Maryse Roudier, who tirelessly assisted with research, crochet and knitting, and photo shoots, and those of technical editor Dorothy Orzel, who meticulously went over patterns, charts, and instructions, and turned out to have an unerring eye for colorful locations as well.

We would like to thank the following people, shops, and institutions who helped us during research and production of this book, especially our agent, Rebecca Davison of Ravenmark, Inc.

We're also grateful to our editor, Betty Wong, for her support for the book.

Test knitters: Alina Badus, Julia Bogardus, Heidi Campbell, Misa Erder, Audrey Honig Geragosian, Mary Hu, Hannah Ingalls, Chawne Kimber, Jenn Wang LaVine, Knit New Haven, Heather McCoy, Katy McCrae, Andrea Mules, Linda Reis, June Sack, Cathy Segal, Rita Zucker.

Models: Marcie Farwell, Raven Julia Juarez Friedman, Sofia Kapur, Holly Kvalheim, Samantha LaVine, Isaiah McLean, Beth Rosenthal, Meghan Schmitt, Vivian Takeuchi, Ellen Van Wyk, Ann Weaver, Emily Zuch.

Photo participants: Brooklyn—Gania Barlow, Alene Latimer; Los Angeles—Lauren Astor, Beth Oliver, Ana Petrova, Carol Precosa, Sarah Redding, Lori Strickler; Seattle—Howlin' Hobbit; Essex Junction, Vermont—Jill Bujold, Helen Bujold, Sophie Bujold, Joan Carver, Shawn Flanigan.

Photo assistance and production: Adrian Bizilia, Gabe Engler-Zucker, Max Mamis, Edwina Stevenson.

Styling and makeup: Kristie Gamer.

Locations and props: Ellen Bloom and Larry Underhill, Victoria Medgyesi, Paul Ray, Maura Shapley and Jack LeNoir, Kaleidoscope Yarns (Essex Junction, Vermont),

National Afro-American Museum and Cultural Center (Wilberforce, Ohio), the Middle East Restaurant and Club (Cambridge, Massachusetts), Watts Towers (Los Angeles, California), Yale University Peabody Museum of Natural History.

Yarn: Berroco, Brown Sheep Company, Cascade Yarns, Knitting Fever International, Louet, Mission Falls, the Schaefer Yarn Company, the Yarnmarket (Pickerington, Ohio).

And, of course, we thank the men who craft our personal communities: Dave Engler and Steve Siegel.

INDEX

NOTE: Page numbers in *italics* indicate projects.

A

Afghans for Afghans, 81, 86, 90, 156
Aids Quilt, 6, 87, 156
Aprons, 71, 156
Arntson, Jenifer Nakatsu, 135
Artise, Bridgett, 107, 156
Artist trading cards (ATCs), 36–43
  about, 37
  Bee Shay and, 36–39, 40, 155
  hosting meeting/exchange, 39
  Serendipity Artist Trading Card, *40–42*
  Web sites, 155
Aspen Invasion—Steamboat Springs, 14
Auerbach, Lisa Anne. *See* Politics, knitting and
Austin Craft Mafia, 134–135

B

Bags
  Granny Greenbag, *77–79*
  from plastic bags (Bags for the People), 115, 156
Bayraktaroglu, Corrine. *See* Knit/yarn bombing (JafaGirls)
Beal, Susan, 135
Bella Brooklyn Housedress, *68–71*
Bench Warmer, *15–19*
Blanket, *90–97*
Bloom, Ellen. *See* Granny squares
Books, 154–155
Brooklyn General *Store*, 64–71
  about, 64, 65–66
  Bella Brooklyn Housedress, *68–71*
  Catherine Clark, Katie Metzger and, 64–67, 156
  Web site, 156

C

Cause, crafting for (knitters united)
  about: overview of, 80–81
  Afghans for Afghans, 81, 86, 90, 156
  Aids Quilt, 6, 87, 156
  Christmas at Sea, 87, 156
  Friends of the Pine Ridge Reservation, 86
  Fussy Cuts Blanket, *90–97*
  Mother Bear Project, 87, 156
  On the Quad Scarf, *88–89*
  Quilts of Valor Foundation, 87, 156
  Red Scarf Project, 82–85, 86, 88–89, 156
  Sleight of Hands Mittens, *98–101*
  Web sites, 156
Chanin, Natalie, 108, 156
Christmas at Sea, 87, 156
Clark, Catherine. *See* Brooklyn General Store
Common Cod Fiber Guild, 134
Community, crafting. *See also* Ravelry phenomenon
  about: overview of, 128–129
  thinking locally, 85

tips for promoting your cause, 85
Coral Reef Project, 31, 155
Cost of handmade items, 23
Coyle, Kat, 142, 156
Craft fairs, organizing, 136
Crafting, getting started, 152
Craftitude Vest, *137 141*
Craft nights, organizing, 75, 156
Crafty Wonderland, 135
Crocheting, 76, 154, 156. *See also* Granny squares
Cross, Lauren, 24, 155
Curtis, Nadine (BeSweet), 108, 156

D

Davis, Lynn, 84
DIY Lounge, 135
DIY movement resources, 155
Dream Rocket, 14
Dresses
  Bella Brooklyn Housedress, *68–71*
  Sun-Tea Dresses, *109–111*

E

Easy-Piecey Peace Quilt, *25–27*
Egan, Mary Lou, 98, 156
Embroidery, 56–63
  Chawne Kimber and, 60, 156
  Hot Stuff Stitching, *61–63*
  Jenny Hart and, 56–59, 61
  Paul Nosa and, 60, 156
  Web sites, 156
Endangered species, 28–35
  big cats and snakes, 29–31
  Coral Reef Project, 31, 155
  knitted *Amur Leopard*, 28, 29
  Laurel Roth and, 31, 155
  Ocelot Scarf, *32–35*
  Ruth Marshall and, 28–31, 32, 155
  Web sites, 155
  Wertheim sisters and, 31
Etsy.com, 23, 59, 134, 152, 156

F

Farwell, Marcie, 66
ffrench, Crispina. *See* Recycling, renewing, and reusing
Fleck, Virginia, 112–114, 116, 156
Fleur de Tin Can, *124–127*
"Flower Power," 11, 12, 14
Forbes, Jessica and Casey, 130–133
Frauenfelder, Mark, 43
Freeman, Roland, 24, 155
Friends of the Pine Ridge Reservation, 86
Fussy Cuts Blanket, *90–97*

G

Gaffey, Theresa, 85
Gardiner, Kay, 90, 156
Geisel, EllynAnne, 71, 156
Gonzalez, Regina Rioux, 76, 156
Granny Greenbag, *77–79*
Granny squares, 72–79
  crochet appeal and, 75, 76
  Ellen Bloom and, 72–75, 77, 156
  Granny Greenbag, *77–79*
  Web sites, 156

H

Hand, Karly, 135
Handmade
  becoming ambassador of, 43
  benefits of, 43
  calculating value of, 23
Hart, Jenny. *See* Embroidery
Hot Stuff Stitching, *61–63*
Howell, Vickie, 135
Hummel, Carol, 14, 155

J

JafaGirls. *See* Knit/yarn bombing (JafaGirls)

K

Kapur, Kristen, 137, 156
Kelly-Landes, Jesse, 135
Keohane, Susann, 135
Kimber, Chawne, 60, 156
Knit Knot Tree, 10, 11
Knitting. *See also* Yarn
  abbreviations, 153
  books, 154
  for causes. *See* Cause, crafting for (knitters united)
  community organizations. *See* Ravelry phenomenon
  endangered species awareness and. *See* Endangered species
  politics and. *See* Politics, knitting and
Knit/yarn bombing (JafaGirls), 10–19
  about, 6, 11–14
  Bench Warmer, *15–19*
  Corrine Bayraktaroglu, Nancy Mellon and, 10–14, 156
  examples, 10, 11–12, 14
  tips for, 13
  Web sites, 155

L

Lee, Jean, 85
Long Day to Starlit Night Wrap, *142–146*
Lounge Act Cardigan, *147–151*
Love, Robyn, 14, 155

M

Magee, Gwendolyn, 24, 155
Marshall, Ruth. *See* Endangered species
Marsh, Jennifer, 14, 155
Maveal, Danielle, 23, 59
Mazloomi, Carolyn, 7, 20-24, 25, 155
Mellon, Nancy. *See* Knit/yarn bombing
    (JafaGirls)
Metzger, Katie. *See* Brooklyn General Store
Miller, Norma, 82-85. *See also* Red Scarf
    Project
Mittens, *98-101*
Mother Bear Project, 87, 156

N

Neitzel, Jen, 135
Nguyen, Torie, 135
Nosa, Paul, 60, 156

O

Ocelot Scarf, *32-35*
On The Quad Scarf, *88-89*
O'Rourke, Rachel, 135
Orphan Foundation of America. *See* Red Scarf
    Project

P

Paper and metalcraft resources, 155. *See also*
    Artist trading cards (ATCs); Toys out of
    trash
Parkes, Clara, 47, 156
Perkins, Hope, 135
Perkins, Jennifer, 134-135
Pitters, Cathy, 135
Plastic, recycling, 112-119
    bags from bags, 115, 156
    making plastic fabric, 114
    Tongue-in-Chic Skirt, *116-119*
    Virginia Fleck and, 112-114, 116, 156
    Web sites, 156
Politics, knitting and, 44-53
    Lisa Anne Auerbach and, 44-47, 48, 156
    Sharrow Cardi, *48-53*
    Take This Knitting Machine and Shove It show
        and, 46, 47
    Web sites, 156
Projects (easy)
    Bench Warmer, *15-19*
    Easy-Piecey Peace Quilt, *25-27*
    Fleur de Tin Can, *124-127*
    Granny Greenbag, *77-79*
    Hot Stuff Stitching, *61-63*
    Long Day to Starlit Night Wrap, *142-146*
    On the Quad Scarf, *88-89*
    Serendipity Artist Trading Card, *40-42*
    Tongue-in-Chic Skirt, *116-119*
Projects (experienced)
    Ocelot Scarf, *32-35*
    Sharrow Cardi, *48-53*

Projects (intermediate)
    Bella Brooklyn Housedress, *68-71*
    Craftitude Vest, *137-141*
    Fussy Cuts Blanket, *90-97*
    Lounge Act Cardigan, *147-151*
    Sleight of Hands Mittens, *98-101*
    Sun-Tea Dresses, *109-111*
Promoting yourself, 59

Q

Quilting, 20-27
    African American history and, 21-23, 24
    Aids Quilt, 6, 87, 156
    Carolyn Mazloomi and, 7, 20-24, 25, 155
    Easy-Piecey Peace Quilt, *25-27*
    Gwendolyn Magee and, 24, 155
    Lauren Cross and, 24, 155
    Quilts of Valor Foundation, 87, 156
    Roland Freeman and, 24, 155
    Web sites, 155
Quilts of Valor Foundation, 87, 156

R

Ravelry phenomenon
    about, 130-133
    Craftitude Vest, *137-141*
    Jessica and Casey Forbes and, 130-133
    Kat Coyle and, 142, 156
    Kristen Kapur and, 137, 156
    Long Day to Starlit Night Wrap, *142-146*
    Lounge Act Cardigan, *147-151*
    other similar communities, 134-135
    Web sites, 156
Recrafting the past, 54-55. *See also* Brooklyn
    General Store; Embroidery; Granny squares
Recycling, renewing, and reusing. *See also*
    Plastic, recycling; Toys out of trash
    about: overview of, 102-103
    Crispina ffrench and, 104-107, 109, 156
    digging for vintage treasures, 107
    Nadine Curtis (BeSweet) and, 108, 156
    Natalie Chanin and, 108, 156
    recycled chic, 104-111, 156
    Sun-Tea Dresses, *109-111*
    Web sites, 156
Red Scarf Project, 82-85, 86, 88-89, 156
Resources
    books, 154-155
    Web, 155-156
    yarn, 155
Roth, Laurel, 31, 155
Rubin, Ann, 81, 86

S

Scarves
    Long Day to Starlit Night Wrap, *142-146*
    Ocelot Scarf, *32-35*
    On the Quad Scarf (Red Scarf Project),
        88-89
Scruggs, Loran. *See* Toys out of trash
Serendipity Artist Trading Card, *40-42*
Sewing resources, 154. *See also* Brooklyn
    General Store; Quilting; Recycling,
    renewing, and reusing
Sharrow Cardi, *48-53*
Shay, Bee. *See* Artist trading cards (ATCs)
Shayne, Ann, 90, 156
Singer, Amy, 75
Skirt, from plastic bags, 116-119
Sleight of Hands Mittens, *98-101*
Sparkles, Tina, 134-135
Statements, crafting, 8-9. *See also* Artist
    trading cards (ATCs); Endangered species;
    Knit/yarn bombing (JafaGirls); Politics,
    knitting and; Quilting
Stein, Guido, 134
Sun-Tea Dresses, *109-111*
Sweaters
    Craftitude Vest, *137-141*
    Lounge Act Cardigan, *147-151*
    Sharrow Cardi, *48-53*

T

Teaching crafts, 67
The Knitted Mile, 14
Tongue-in-Chic Skirt, *116-119*
Toys out of trash, 120-127
    finding tins for, 122
    Fleur de Tin Can, *124-127*
    Loran Scruggs and, 120-124, 156

V

Valuing handmade items, 23
Vintage treasures, 107

W

Weaver, Ann, 147, 156
Web resources, 155-156
Werker, Kim, 76, 156
Wertheim, Christine and Margaret, 31
Wrap, *142-146*
Wudowsky, Claire, 85

Y

Yarn. *See also* Knit/yarn bombing (JafaGirls);
    Knitting
    resources, 155
    weight chart, 153
    writing with, 47

FOR DAVE, LEO, GABE, AND STEVE

Published in the United States by Potter Craft,
an imprint of the Crown Publishing Group,
a division of Random House, Inc., New York.
www.crownpublishing.com
www.pottercraft.com
POTTER CRAFT and colophon
is a registered trademark of Random House, Inc.

Library of Congress Cataloging-in-Publication Data
        Tapper, Joan.
        Craft activism : People, ideas, and projects from the new community of handmade and
how you can join in / Joan Tapper, Gale Zucker ; [foreword by] Faythe Levine. — 1st ed.
            p. cm.
        Includes bibliographical references.
        ISBN-13: 978-0-307-58662-9 (pbk.)
        ISBN-10: 0-307-58662-6 (pbk.)
        1. Handicraft. 2. Social movements. I. Zucker, Gale. II. Title.
        TT149.T37 2011
        745.5—dc22
                                2011003675

Printed in China
Design by Kara Plikaitis & Jess Morphew
Photography by Gale Zucker
Photos on page 20, bottom left and right, courtesy Carolyn Mazloomi
Photo on page 28, upper left, courtesy Ruth Marshall
Photo on page 46 courtesy Lisa Anne Auerbach
Technical editing by Dorothy Orzel
Thanks to the Craft Yarn Council of America
for its Standard Yarn Weight System chart,
which appears on p. 153

10 9 8 7 6 5 4 3 2 1
First Edition